CW00937737

paint it black

black

A Guide to Gothic Homemaking

VOLTAIRE

WEISER BOOKS
Boston, MA/York Beach, ME

First published in 2005 by
Red Wheel/Weiser, LLC
York Beach, ME
With offices at:
368 Congress Street
Boston, MA 02210
www.redwheelweiser.com

Library of Congress Cataloging-in-Publication Data
Voltaire.
    Paint it black : a guide to Gothic homemaking / Voltaire.
       p. cm.
    ISBN 1-57863-361-3 (alk. paper)
    1. Goth culture (Subculture)—Humor.
    2. Interior decoration—Humor. I.
Title.
  PN6231.G75V65 2005
  818'.607—dc22
                                              2005014210

Cover: Lilah & Voltaire • Photo: Nadya Lev • Design: Tallulah Blackhead
Typeset in Adobe Garamond by Tallulah Blackhead

Printed in Canada
Friesens

12 11 10 09 08 07 06 05
  8 7 6 5 4 3 2 1

table of contents

introduction

Three Decades and Some Odd Years o
Painting It Black

S FAR BACK AS I CAN REMEMBER I HAVE BEEN
AN OF THE MACABRE. IT STARTED SO LONG AGO, I
ACT, THAT I DIDN'T EVEN HAVE A NAME FOR IT UNTI
Y LATER YEARS; I WASN'T OLD ENOUGH THE
differentiate between horror, science fiction, and fantasy—and
dn't matter much. I solely knew that I loved "monsters." I just wa
rawn to all strange creatures and the strange, exotic worlds in whic
ey lived. I spent countless hours watching "monster movies"—as
lled them—enveloped in a desire to escape to a fantastic realr
ch as theirs. A dark, romantic place filled with mystery and dram
land far-removed and completely unlike the unbearably mundar
ation in which I lived: the sprawling suburbs of New Jersey.

By the age of ten, I had stumbled upon the films of Ra
arryhausen (*Jason and the Argonauts, The 7th Voyage of Sinbac*
d was instantly swept away! The creatures in his films seemed s
riously real to me. They were not men in rubber suits trashin
niature sets of Tokyo. They were clearly not actors in capes wit
tmeal on their faces. They weren't marionettes on strings. I had n
ea what magic it was that brought them to life. Like a ten-year-ol
ad scientist, I wanted desperately to unravel that mystery. I ever
ally came to learn that this *magic* was called stop-motion anima
n. I knew from that point that I wanted to be a stop-motion an
itor when I grew up. I bought a Super 8 camera and began exper
enting, making stop-motion films in the basement of my mother
use. I started reading magazines like *Fangoria*, *Starlog* and
nemagic in the hopes of learning how to build rubber models and
mate them. Through making movies, I taught myself how t
ke molds, cast rubber, build sets, and paint them. (These tech

niques would serve me later on in my interior design endeavors.

If one were to conduct a psychological evaluation of *why* I loved monsters so much, one might uncover my deep-seated distrust of "normal" people. I was surrounded by people who appeared to be "good" but always seemed to want to do me harm. On the other hand, monsters were always very honest: they looked bad and they were bad. There was no deception, no subterfuge.

Furthermore, my desire to make animated films could be regarded as a need to create alternate worlds to which I could escape, breaking free from the unhappy one in which I lived. Luckily though, I never much cared for psychoanalysis, so we'll just say that I had found something that interested me.

Eventually the line between my films and my daily life became blurred. At 13, after much begging and pleading, my mother granted me permission to move out of the bedroom I shared with my brother and to take up residence in a small room in the basement; after all, I was "becoming a young man." I cleared out all of the detritus that filled the former storage space and moved in my bed, a night table, a small black and white TV, and a couch.

I felt an inherent need to decorate the room and make it my own. Somehow the *Star Wars* theme that pervaded my previous quarters (i.e., *Star Wars* bed sheets, pillow cases, pajamas, underwear, etc.) just wasn't going to do. I needed to create my *own* world.

If you were to step into a time machine, go back to the fall of 1980, and pay a visit to my new bedroom in the basement of our suburban home, you would probably be horrified to find that I had decorated the entire room in tin foil! Hey, it was as close as I could get to sci-fi chic! The walls, the night table, *all* of the furniture were covered in the wrinkly, silver stuff giving the room the look of a bad sci-fi B-movie (call it "Plan 9-and-a-Half From Outer Space"). I even spray-painted some cardboard boxes silver and decorated them with buttons and levers and such to give them the appearance of control panels. Ed Wood would have been proud.

Nevertheless, I eventually tired of living aboard this low-budget spaceship (especially since it was obviously never going to actually help me escape from New Jersey) and thusly found myself redecorating my room in a different theme every couple of months.

Among the more notable concepts there was a "Satanic Heavy Metal" theme (thank goodness that one didn't last long!). I replaced all of the white bulbs in the room with red ones, giving the room a deep crimson glow. Images of Baphomet and pentagrams lovingly besmirched the walls, and a massive metal incense burner served as the altar on which I performed my "satanic" rituals.

Oh yes! You heard me right, girlfriend! I took my themes *very* seriously! I spent some time at my junior high school library where I checked out books on devils, demons, and the occult, Aleister Crowley, and Anton Szandor LaVey. But of course, like most disenfranchised thirteen-year-olds, I didn't *actually* have any idea what I was doing. I just sort of play-acted what I thought might be effective. You know, rituals to the effect of waving a rabbit's foot key-chain from K-Mart over an incense burner from Spencer Gifts while chanting the names of kids at school who had beat me up. That sort of thing. I probably should have known that I was wasting my time, though, because every time I told my mother I was performing a demonic ritual in the basement, she answered with a blasé, "That's nice, dear."

Well, eventually the satanic theme had to go—probably around the time I realized that those naïve "satanic rituals" were no more effective at smiting my enemies than that busted old tin foil spaceship had been at taking me to outer space.

Other themes over the years included a "Zen Room" motif, a "Haunted Jungle" phase, and a "Dark Hippie" period (I didn't know at the time that the "Dark Hippie" thing was called Goth). But in the end, I settled on a romantic, French red-light district theme: red lights, incense, lots of candles, and empty bottles of cheap red wine stolen from the garbage can (not to mention lots of steamy, adolescent, red-light behavior! Ah, good times . . .).

At seventeen, following the biggest, baddest, and last drag-out with the parents regarding some I-don't-know-what-that-I've-long-since-stopped-caring-about, I moved to Manhattan. Shortly thereafter, I found gainful employment as a stop-motion animator working on television commercials. During the years that followed I learned quite a bit about model making, building sets and props, painting faux finishes, and other such arts. These techniques would

added to my arsenal of skills for turning drab living spaces int
ntastic locales.

At one point during the 1990s, I was living in a Lower East Sid
nement apartment. The place was really raw and had no electricit
ing mostly found objects, though, I was able to transform the plac
to an enchanted magical forest in the heart of th
wish/Dominican ghetto ("I'll have the Matzo ball soup with a sid
fried plantains, please").

The ceiling was covered with an enormous painting of a tumultuou
y from a Hieronymus Bosch painting (created in the '80s for th
ackdrop of an MTV station ID I had directed). A great, white mo
aito net hung over the bed. The walls were painted with a rusti
pia faux finish replete with cracks (most of them real) and fossils (a
them fake). The walls were also trimmed with dozens of bouque
dried roses (fished from the trash) in addition to branches that bur
t from the walls and reached up towards the stormy ceiling. Th
nk and countertop were covered in moss and only served as a hon
two turtles, Romeo and Juliet (I washed the dishes in the tub
rickets purchased at the local pet store to feed my pets roame
eely, filling the flat with their song. And the whole of this fantast
orld was lit by hundreds of candles burning in "bottle candelabra
nd in wall-mounted boxes.

New Yorkers are notorious for throwing out perfectly good cra
nd so whenever I would find a discarded cabinet on the street
hich was often—I would remove the drawers, bring them hom
nd nail them to the walls. They served as shelving and simultan
usly made everything one put in them seem like works of art.

The one and only electrical device in my residence was a batter
perated cassette player that exclusively played Japanese Koto a
hai Gamelan tapes. Visitors would come over and marvel at ho
nuch the place felt like a nighttime forest even though it was indoo

During my years in that apartment, I also used my knowledge
culpting and prop-making to make plaster statuary, candleholde
nd macabre sketchbooks that looked like ancient grimoires. I so
hem to local Goth shops to supplement my income during a ti
hen the growing popularity of computer animation made it de

near impossible to find work as a stop-motion animator. But, ne ess to say, the surplus plaster statuary added to the ancient, outd garden-look of the place.

Most would find the desire to transform one's living space in su a dramatic way a bit odd, to say the least; for me, though, it's alw been a given. I simply have always felt a need to make my surrou ng environment one in which I would want to live, regardless how strange it might appear to others.

People constantly ask me what inspires me. I tell them that I a nspired by idiocy, mediocrity, and garbage. I survey the wo around me and wonder how we came to live in such a boring a mundane culture. I turn on the radio and hear crap. I turn on the t evision (now that I have electricity) and wonder why there is no ng worth watching on the 500-plus channels cable has to of except for Star Trek, of course!). I go to the mall looking for Edw Gorey but all I find is Eddie Bauer.

What happened to the romance and pageantry of the past? Ho did we come to live in a world inundated by blue jeans and kha and baseball caps, where the average person dresses like a mechar or farmer or baseball player? These days, why is it that the only pe le holding dearly to the elegance of the past are Hasidic Jews, t Amish, and us Goths?

Whether it was animation, comics, music, or my immediate su oundings, I realized long ago that if it doesn't exist, I simply have make it myself. I have learned to take the horribly mundane and tu t into the wonderfully macabre; and to this end I have created *Pai t Black*. Unlike its predecessor, *What Is Goth?*, this book is in essen "how-to" book. Within its pages you will find techniques for cr ting spooky toys, gothic decorations, and macabre objets d'art. ives me great pleasure to share some of these concoctions with yo nd I hope they will aid you in creating an alternative world to li a place in which to celebrate the dark, the romantic, and the wor

goth 101 and beyond

Deconstructing Goth from the Catacombs Up

THE BIG QUESTION IS "WHAT IS GOTH?" AND IT IS A LOADED QUESTION INDEED.

Luckily the predecessor to this book is titled just that and covers a large range of territory in answering that question. So, for a thorough (and often truly silly) take on the topic, I recommend you give that book a read. But here, for the purposes of understanding Gothic decorating, we will examine the foundation of the culture's visual aesthetics.

ESSENTIAL GOTH

On the subject of Goth decorating, there are a few simple standards that if adhered to will help you to turn just about anything Goth.

Step One: Paint It Black

For starters: *paint it black.* (Yes, I do have a knack for the obvious when it comes to naming books.)

Goth as a musical subgenre came to be in the late '70s and early '80s on the heels of Punk. While Punk was angry and rebellious, Goth was its more introspective offspring chiefly concerned with looking within at the true nature of the human condition. Gothic music—back then, at least—leaned towards melancholy and emotional themes. The movement has come to be generally categorized as an appreciation for the romantic, the emotional, and the dark. And no color quite captures the concept of darkness quite like the color black.

In essence, black tends to be the principal color used in all things Goth; hence, the act of painting something black brings you a step closer to achieving the gothic aesthetic. (Paint your toenails black and you're half way there.)

There are certain images that, for one reason or another, have been adopted by the gothic movement. At the top of the list are skulls.

The popularly held notion that skulls are somehow evil or satanic is ludicrous to Goths (and should be to all). Goths know that skulls are harmless. Everyone's got one. And it's a damn good thing. If you didn't have a skull in your head, you probably would not have made it past the age of three without experiencing some measure of brain damage.

Perhaps the fascination with skulls is born of the Goth impulse to examine the human condition, a state that invariably ends in death. To a Goth, happy-go-lucky people who never think of death are in essence deluding themselves. It's the inevitable conclusion—but not necessarily a negative one. In accepting and understanding that death is the inescapable end, one is forced to truly examine and evaluate *life*, and thus our existence and purpose on this orb. And any thorough exploration of our purpose is bound to lead to at least a momentary bout of melancholia.

But it's probably truer to say that Goths love skulls because they freak the hell out of everyone else!

Encountering human remains is *never* a pleasant thing and even a hardcore Goth would have to confess to a sudden loosening of the bowels if they were to have such an encounter. However, in our present day and age, it is extremely rare that any of us will ever stumble across an actual human skull. That was not always the case. In less civilized times it was perhaps not uncommon to find human remains lying about after a war or a plague. In short, ages ago, coming across a skull was a harbinger of impending doom. Thus it came to be that seeing a skull struck fear in the hearts of humanity—and justifiably so.

irates caught on to this and terrorized their victims by flying th olly Roger. Later in human history, the skull and crossbones becam n international symbol for something extremely harmful to you ealth (poison for instance). These days, however, this symbol is li e more than a mere image.

Basically, Goths wear skulls because they think they look cool. An erhaps, subconsciously to some Goths, wearing images of skul ommunicates, "I think about death." That's all innocent enough Doctors think about death, too . . . as do racecar drivers, astronaut nd most definitely life insurance salesmen.

But to my fellow Goths I say, have a little patience with the no nals. They don't quite get it. They are a little bit stuck on the syn olism. When they see you coming, they don't think, "Oh, cool sku -shirt." The thought that runs through their minds is, "Oh n Here's comes a big, black, spiky-haired bottle of death!"

Step Three: Release the Bats!

o, to make something Goth, paint it black and slap a skull on it.

I could end right there; but if I did I'd just make you and all our belongings look like you fell off of a pirate ship. Of cours hat's not *completely* bad. Goths love visiting places like Ne Orleans, San Diego, Barbados (all places where it really sucks to l ressed in black vinyl, I might add), and just about anywhere el vith a port, the reason being that these spots are prone to havir ons of pirate-themed souvenirs for tourists. They are some of th *nly* places where a Goth can easily find a shirt that suits his or h aste. And any Goth will tell you that you can *never* have too mar lack t-shirts with skulls on them.

But Goth is much more than looking like an overzealous Oaklan[d] [R]aiders fan. Beyond the fascination with skulls is a love for all thing[s] [b]atty.

The bat has been the unofficial mascot of Goth right from the ver[y] [b]eginnings of the movement. All of the genre's seminal band[s] [B]auhaus, Siouxsie and the Banshees, The Cure) got their start at [a] [L]ondon club called the Batcave. The fact that these bands style[d] [th]emselves after characters from gothic horror movies furthe[r] [ce]mented the Goth affinity for bats. Moreover, on a subconsciou[s] [le]vel perhaps, Goths see the bat as a creature whose lifestyle is ana[lo]gous to their own.

Bats are nocturnal. Goths are nocturnal.

Bats are harmless, yet feared. Goths are as well.

Bats primarily eat fruit and insects . . . okay, never mind.

So, yeah. Paint it black, slap a skull on it, and also infest it with [a co]lony of bats for good measure. (Add some spider webs and you'[re] *really* rockin' it!). And *that*, dear friends, is (or can be) the whol[e] [of] Goth 101.

Every Day Is Halloween

[O]f course, you don't need to stop at bats and skulls. Most Goths ten[d to] love all things macabre. Naturally then, Halloween is every Goth'[s] [fa]vorite holiday. Devils and demons and spiders and mummie[s] [ra]vens and crows and rats and tarantulas, big spooky skeletons hang[in]g from strings, these are just some of our favorite things!

If it's an image you are likely to come across on Halloween [ch]ances are it's something you can add to your gothic decoratin[g] [im]age bank. And the operative words here are "come across," as it'[s] [hi]ghly likely that even the most sickeningly mainstream and com[m]ercial store at the mall will have a plethora of spooky items from [wh]ich to choose come Halloween. Thus, late October 'tis the seaso[n] [fo]r Goths to go shopping! While the rest of the world is buying cos[tu]mes they will wear once and then discard or is putting up fright[en]ing decorations that will be defenestrated on the AM of Novembe[r] [1s]t, thousands of Goths are purchasing their wardrobes for the year [It] is also a great time to load up on gothic home decorating supplie[s] like spider webs, plastic skulls, artificial creeper vines, Styrofoam tombstones, plastic gargoyles, and the like.

So, stock up around Halloween-time and your abode will be wonderfully horrific all year long.

However, if you happen to live in a major city, you may be lucky enough to have one or two costume shops or Halloween stores that are open all year long. In Manhattan, I spend a lot of time at a massive shop called Halloween Adventure shopping for sundry spooky items year round. It's kind of like a gothic megamart. It's not uncommon for me to run into other Goths doing some weekend shopping. "Excuse me, Vlad, could you pass the rubber bats?" A Goth promoter whom I work with in Japan, Taiki-san (DJ Grimoire), travels to New York an average of three or four times a year from Japan to stock up on spooky decorations at Halloween Adventure for his shop, home, and events. Domo Arigato, Mr. Gothboto!

And don't forget, short of having a year-round Halloween shop near you, there's always the World Wide Web (no, not spider web, silly!).

IT'S A GOTH WORLD AFTER ALL

Of course to end at the above list of motifs would be an over simplification, and unfortunately Goth is just not that simple. Here are some other sources from which you can cull Gothic elements.

The West

As an aesthetic, Goth does not draw from any particular time period or style. Because romance and antiquity are at the core of what is Goth, the genre incorporates elements of countless different epochs, eras, and places. Romantigoths go to great lengths to capture the dark elegance of Victorian England; just as readily, they may draw from the Renaissance or from medieval times.

Also, Goths are not opposed to employing religious iconography despite their usually paradoxical religious views. Rather, they do so endeavoring to capture the weight and melancholy found in religious images of tortured saints, martyrs, etc. Come to think of it, the Catholic Church did invent some of the most grotesquely sinister torture devices ever conceived by man! So, naturally—and perhaps not so ironically—the Gothic period (in architecture and art) is drawn upon heavily even though it consisted of loads of religious imagery.

And so, you might see a Goth wearing a medieval bodice with a Victorian bustle skirt with jewelry bearing ancient Egyptian hieroglyphs. But like an old Ray Harryhausen film (where a Cyclops fights a Griffin fights a Hindu goddess), it all just seems to work.

Cyber

I must mention that not all Goths are enamored of the past. CyberGoths prefer to look to the future. They take their aesthetic inspirations from an imagined future—one in which humans are part machine, hair is made of brightly-colored synthetic fibers, all of mankind march fervently in step to a colossal drum machine . . . and where glowsticks are somehow *not* dorky Raver gear.

A CyberGoth's apartment is less likely to be adorned with skulls and bats and far more likely to be sleek and mechanical, decorated with robot toys, spiky latex furniture, and lots and lots of rubber or vinyl tubing. Store all of your stuff in plastic boxes from Staples or Home Depot (*don't* cover them with black satin) and none of your CyberGoth friends will blink a synthetic eyelash.

If you are a CyberGoth, chances are you are just as interested in the Styrofoam material that your computer came packed in as you are with the computer itself: with a little acrylic paint and some rubber tubing, you can easily turn it into a wonderfully cyber wall-hanging.

Some Goths borrow elements from Asian cultures. Black and orange or black and red—combinations that very much appeal to Goths—are prevalent color schemes in Chinese art and design. Standing before a blood red, wooden bed frame intricately carved with images of dragons and demons, there is no denying its intrinsic gothic value. Walk into ABC Carpet and Home in Manhattan and in their Chinese antiques department you will find Chinese furniture most Goths would kill for (and most of us will never be able to afford).

But Chinese Goth can also be done on the cheap. Go to any Chinatown and you will find reasonably priced red Chinese lanterns or simple and elegant rice paper lanterns that won't break the bank. While there, pick up some black dragon statues (cast in resin or plastic) to give your home a dark and worldly look. Moreover, they will give your words a touch of authenticity when you proclaim, "Yeah, I've been a vampire now for two thousand years. I picked up these knick-knacks in the 6th Century while terrorizing Shanghai."

Most shops in Chinatown will also have a variety of clothes from which to choose. Get yourself a black, silk cheongsam and a black lacquered fan; they will instantly transform you into the reigning Dragon Lady at the Gothic prom. If you're a guy, style yourself in an elegant Chinese jacket. Hey, it worked for Rogue from the Cruxshadows! (Caution: if you're not a rock star, don't walk around with the wireless mic or else you'll look like you're taking orders at a Chinese fast-food restaurant. "Okay, so that's one Chiang Kai-shek value meal with an extra egg roll. Got it!")

With its elegant simplicity in blacks, whites, and reds, Japanese design is another Goth favorite. Again, dragons and paper lanterns are definitive elements, although they may be harder to find in Japanese styles and most likely will be more expensive.

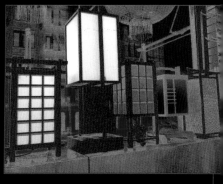

The rampant popularity of Japanese animation (Anime) has also fed the flames of interest. Films like *Vampire Hunter D, Vampire Princess Miyu, The Ghost in the Shell, Blood: The Last Vampire,* etc., have opened Western Goths' eyes to the possibilities of incorporating Japanese aesthetics in their Gothic garb and decorating ventures.

It has even become increasingly common for young American girls interested in both Goth and Anime to take on Japanese names (in life or just online). There isn't a day that goes by that I don't get an email from some "Usagi Hime" (Rabbit Princess) or "Chibi Yoko-chan" (Little Yoko) who turns out to be a thirteen-year-old white girl named Gertrude from Heath, Ohio.

At any rate, Japanese styles do lend themselves to Gothic decorating and dress and, if done well, can really make you the "Koomori No Kisaki" (Bat Queen) of the ball. For example, kimonos are easy to come by and are absolutely, ravishingly elegant when worn correctly. The Gothic Geisha look is rarely done and is always a big hit.

Please though, do us both a favor and avoid using the word "geisha" if you don't *really* know what one is. Sadly, Americans seem to think that all Japanese women wearing traditional dress are referred to as "geishas." I assure you this is not the case. A geisha is essentially a courtesan; so, unless you sincerely *mean* to say that you are rigorously trained and highly skilled in the art of entertaining men, avoid invoking the word. You would in essence be saying that you are an expensive call girl.

Weaponry also abounds at Japanese gift shops. It can make for a nice decorative ingredient; but make sure to use it in moderation. Fill your home with samurai swords and you will basically look like the Japanese equivalent of a "gun nut." And no one, but no one, loves a gun nut . . . above the Mason Dixon line, at least. Furthermore, no matter how cool they may look with your outfit, avoid bringing swords to clubs or events unless they are "peace bonded," (if you are a boffer geek you will know what I'm talking about).

Goth Tiki?

I recently went to a Deathrock party in New York City called "Curse of the Hearse." It was held at a tiki bar by the name of Otto's Shrunken Head. The DJs, Allison and Fritz, were spinning '80s deathrock tunes. At one point, I looked up at the video monitor to see *The Island of Lost Souls* playing. I sat there sipping my Red Devil out of a spooky tiki mug in a room adorned with skulls when it suddenly hit me: Goth Tiki! I remember this!

Who would have guessed that Tiki could be Goth? Well actually your grandparents might have! In the 1930s, American filmmakers tapped into a genre that filled audiences with an ominous sense of dread. Many action and suspense films during that era were set in the jungles of Southeast Asia, Polynesia, and Africa where the wilds are thick, very very dark, and filled with exotic and unexpected dangers. Add to that backdrop foreboding scores with low-register, bowel loosening horns and Afro-Cuban rhythms and you have a truly dark (if not classically Gothic) experience.

You won't generally find vampires in these films, but you will find plenty of other creepy characters. Some of my favorite films from that era are *King Kong*, *Son of Kong* and the aforementioned *Island of Lost Souls.*

Even Betty Boop joined in the trend. Watch some of the early Betty Boop cartoons and you will see her being spirited away to dark jungles by man-eating cannibals intent on picking a bone with her (or *from* her). Southeast Asian, African, and Tiki motifs may seem like an odd choice for a Goth, but consider this: wherever there are cannibals (real or imaginary), there are skulls . . . lots and lots of skulls (for an explanation of why skulls are Goth, go back to the beginning of this section).

Stuff that will make your room look like a vampire tiki bar include: skulls, voodoo dolls, tiki mugs, big artificial vines and creepers, anything made out of bamboo, and a well placed rubber snake or two. Pirate or sailor paraphernalia might come in handy and a life-sized skeleton is always a nice touch; dress him up like Gilligan (from *Gilligan's Island*) for some extra yuks.

Tiki hails specifically from Polynesia (Hawaii, Bikini, etc); but there is nothing keeping you from throwing in whatever fits your fancy that seems vaguely related to the concept. You would not be the first to wing it. It's not uncommon for people to throw in elements from other cultures in the neighborhood—like Malaysia, Thailand, or Indonesia—despite the fact that there is nothing Tiki about them. For example, the original *King Kong* (1933) takes place on some remote island in Southeast Asia, but all of the natives are black. They must have had some truly awesome canoes 'cause it's a *long* way from Africa to Borneo!

Death—Indonesian Style

Indonesia has its own very unique style. It's rarely used in Gothic decorating—which is surprising because so much of the culture's art is spooky and macabre. Walk into a shop that sells Indonesian crafts and you will instantly be surrounded by colorful wooden sculptures of winged frogs, bats, and odd little angels with white eyes. Most are designed to hang in a flying position from the ceiling. My favorites are the flying mermaids with pale skin and hollow eyes, perpetually staring blankly into mirrors while combing their long, flowing hair. They are all together beautiful and haunting. And yes, they are colorful. But don't worry: while occasionally vibrant, the colors used tend to be lush secondary and tertiary shades

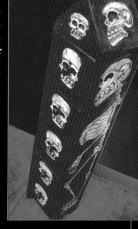

that even a Goth would be proud to display in their lair.

You can also find some intricately carved wooden statues of Garudas—that is, really horrifyingly fierce half-bird half-human creatures.

But most importantly, you can find a wide array of black boxes in all shapes and sizes

adorned with skulls and skeletons carved out of wood. And, once again, you can never go wrong with skulls.

BLACK TO THE BASICS

In any culture, period, or style of art you will find *something* that conveys that feeling of romance, dark elegance, or sweet melancholy that is Goth. If you don't already have a nose for such spooky stuff, rest assured that it will come with time (especially if you spend lots of time at Goth clubs or with that same nose stuck in copies of *Gothic Beauty* magazine).

I could go on and on about all of the different elements or motifs you could employ to make something Goth, because the fact of the matter is that Goth is less defined by what it is than what it is not. Truth be told, in the world of Gothic decorating, the sky is the limit (as long as that sky is dark, grey, and overcast).

But at the end of the day, if in doubt, paint it black and slap a skull on it.

The worst that can happen is that someone will walk up to you and say, "Arrrrr, matey!"

the tools of destruction

. . . Are the Weapons of Creation

As we venture into the realm of gothic homemaking, there are a few items you will need in order to gothify the mundane. Allow me to introduce you to the tools of the trade:

BLACK SPRAY PAINT

I call it "The Gothilizer!" You can just call it ultra flat black spray paint. Coat just about any commonplace object with it and you are nine-tenths of the way to making said object look Goth. Personally I prefer the brand Krylon; but you can use what you like.

Some words of caution:

You should *always* use spray paint in a well-ventilated area; by that I mean either in a spray booth or (preferably) outside. Inhaling spray paint fumes is hazardous to your health. Painting something black is Goth. Painting your lungs black is just plain stupid, so please avoid it at all costs.

Also keep in mind that while spraying you are going to inadvertently paint the area around the object. Make sure to lay down plenty of paper, even if outside—there are better ways to "paint the town black" than by accident.

Furthermore, bear in mind that spray paint can have a very strong smell (i.e., stinks like the devil).

So, make sure to let whatever you paint air out before bringing it back into your home. When visitors ask you, "What's that smell?" the correct answer is *supposed* to be "patchouli."

THE GLUE GUN

If you have never used a glue gun before, then I am honored to introduce you to a tool that is going to make you Gother than you could ever imagine. Why, you ask? Well, I have been using glue guns for nearly twenty years now and I have never met a glue gun-user (including myself) who hasn't at some point squirted a heaping dollop of blazing hot, molten glue into the palm of his or her hand. And let me tell you that as Goth as you think you are, you have *never* known the unfathomable depths of excruciating anguish and despair than will be revealed to you when you've done this (and chances are that you will, if you're not *extremely* careful). And if you think that having molten glue in your hand sucks, try peeling it off . . . with a couple layers of your skin attached to it. Suffice to say, nothing else you've experienced in your wretched life will be as shite-poem inspiring as this hellish experience.

That having been said, here's how a hot glue gun works. First, plug it in. A hot glue gun is basically a heater; it warms up and the tip in particular gets extremely hot. Next, insert a glue stick. When you pull the trigger (or push the stick in with your hand—depending on which make and model you buy), it comes out the other end as hot, liquid glue. The fact that the stick goes in as a solid and comes out as a liquid should clue you in on how hot it gets.

In short, this is a great and marvelous tool that you will find extremely useful for countless art projects. However, use it with caution or else your sucky life will become a whole lot suckier.

And as with any tool that gets hot, keep an eye on it and don't set your house on fire. Fun stuff, huh?

In short, this is glue in an aerosol can. I like Super 77 by 3M, but there are lots of spray adhesives on the market from which you can choose.

The really nice thing about this stuff is that you can turn anything into a sticker! Take a photograph, a drawing, a patch, or a page from a magazine, spray the back and voilà, you can stick it to just about any surface.

There are two ways in which I use spray adhesive:

- Spray it onto something (like the back of a photo) and then to stick said object to something else (like a bottle).

- Use it as a contact cement. Spray both surfaces that you wish to bind, wait for them to dry, and then press them together. It doesn't sound like it should work, but for magical reasons that elude my nonscientific mind, they stick to one another like crazy.

As with any spray, you want to do this outside. Besides being harmful if inhaled, spray adhesive has a tendency to get all over the place. If you spray it indoors—even if you put down paper—it gets in the air, drifts across the room, and settles elsewhere. Wherever it lands, it makes the surface tacky (like, say, on your favorite black velvet cape). Subsequently, all of the dust and lint in the air will stick to it, creating a very nasty mess that's nearly impossible to clean.

Oh, and by the way—contrary to popular belief, Rogue from the Cruxshadows does *not* use spray adhesive to get his hair to stand up like that . . . and neither should you!

Yes, girls often run around in Goth clubs sporting bikini tops made of black electrical tape. It's a fine look. Hell, it's a great look! But did you know that black electrical tape had other uses—well, besides the obvious application (which I'm *guessing* has something do with electrical mumbo jumbo or whatnot)? This stuff can really come in handy when you are Gothing-up a household item or toy. I've been using it for years on my stop-motion animation models.

For example, simply wrap it around a doll's legs and arms and you will swear that they are wearing PVC clothes. And you don't even need to know how to sew! It's an insta-fetish look right at your fingertips.

Alright, Bat-man (or Bat-girl). Now you have the basic tools in your Gothic utility belt. Go forth and transform the mundane into the macabre!

gothic decorating: the basics

Dressing Your Room with Sumptuous Gloom

YOU HAVE A BARE ROOM WITH WHITE WALLS. HOW DO YOU MAKE IT GOTH?

Living in Manhattan, I tend to move every few years (I'm not sure why but it seems to be a universal affliction in this city). Thus, I have had many opportunities to turn small, bare spaces into lairs worthy of a character from a Bram Stoker novel.

Listed below are some techniques that you can employ to do the same.

THE WALLS CRAWL

Think of your room as an oversized diorama. Before you can fill it with wonderfully Gothic decor, you need to set the mood by painting the walls. Choose a color that will best suit your purposes.

Red Walls

No matter how you slice it, it's really really hard to Goth-out a room that has white walls. Having a rich, romantic color to work with is equivalent to priming a canvas. In my opinion, the best base color for a soon-to-be-Goth room is red. But stay away from primary red. You want your room to look romantic and hot—as in sultry—not like a fire engine. Steer towards secondary shades of red, like crimson or burgundy. Also, red paint names that bear an Oriental title tend to work nicely.

Personally, I'm a fan of Benjamin Moore's Exotic Red, which is the color of my present apartment. It covered really effectively with only one coat and is so lovely that little else has been needed to make the place look great.

(Here's a frighteningly fun fact: There are those in the world of science who believe that red walls will cause a person to eventually go insane. Cool!)

Black Walls

Resist the temptation to paint the walls black! I can tell you from experience that if you are starting with a smallish room, painting the walls black will make the room look even smaller. Furthermore, it will eventually depress you to a point far beyond the usual "I'm so Goth I'm dead . . . aren't I wonderfully mysterious?" to a stage where you will actually need to seek serious and immediate professional attention.

You can ignore this rule if you plan to fill the room with black lights and cover the walls with UV posters. But still, turning your room into a corner of a Spencer Gifts store is wrong for a whole other set of reasons I shouldn't have to go into. And besides, if you spend too much time under black lights, you'll be blind within a year . . . in which case *all* you'll see is black. Awesome!

Antique Walls

Faux finishes are also a nice touch. Since Goth draws from so many sources (most of them bygone eras), giving the room a rustic, ancient look can also prove to be very complimentary. Ancient Roman, Greek, Moroccan, or Egyptian themes are all motifs that you can employ.

In my previous apartment this rusticity was a great look and worked excellently. I lived in a *really* dilapidated, pre-war tenement apartment building on the Lower East Side; the walls were so distraught and had been painted over so many times that they resembled a topographical map of Africa. To enhance this, I painted the walls a warm, autumny yellow. Once that had dried, I slapped a darker sepia color onto the walls, which I wiped off with a damp towel while it was still slightly wet. The darker paint got into all of the crevices but was completely removed from the flatter, raised portions, giving the walls a deceivingly timeworn look.

If you live in a more modern space with perfectly flat walls you can achieve a similarly distressed effect by painting the walls one color and, once dry, patting a darker or lighter shade of the same color onto the walls with a dry sponge. Simply dip the sponge into a bit of paint and then pat it several times on a newspaper until the paint is almost dry. Then, lightly dab the sponge all over the wall to apply a light speckling of paint. Irregularly shaped sea sponges work best and give you a more random pattern than regular sponges. You might want to experiment with this technique first on a piece of paper or hidden piece of wall (behind a couch or in a closet) until you get the desired effect.

If you like, you can even simulate cracks by painting them in with a fine brush or by placing some paint on the edge of a trowel or palette knife and running it along the wall. In my previous abode I even painted fossils on the wall. Remember, this is supposed to look like ancient Rome, and like they say, "when in Rome . . . draw fossils on the wall."

(Did you know? Yellow walls are said to be calming—something that really comes in handy on the Lower East Side where you can hear a day-long chorus of police sirens, screams, and the occasional gunfire. Ah, yellow. Suddenly I feel at ease.)

White Walls

If you absolutely can't paint your walls any color other than white (e.g., it's your parents home and they won't stand for it, or perhaps your landlord is a Nazi) simply cover as much surface as you can with posters, prints, or paintings. Turn-of-the-century prints (reproductions, of course), like the *Tournee du Chat Noir*, by Theophile Alexandre Steinlen, or images depicting scenes from 19th Century Parisian nightlife, like those of Henri de Toulouse-Lautrec, will add a refined Gothy touch.

If the archetypal Gothic teenager room is more your speed, cover your walls with posters of your favorite bands. Catch the Cruxshadows when they are in your town and stock up on what they have to offer. Or go online and procure some posters of London After Midnight, The Cure, Siouxsie and the Banshees, Bauhaus, etc.

Movie posters can also do the job, and there are plenty of favorite films from which you can choose: *The Nightmare Before Christmas*, *The Crow*, *Edward Scissorhands*, *Dracula*, *The Hunger* . . . you get the picture (literally).

Fabric Walls

Curtains: they're not just for windows anymore!

Since the dawn of time—okay, maybe just since the Middle Ages—kings have adorned their walls with tapestries. If you can't or don't wish to paint your walls, consider following royalty's example and conceal them with flowing fabrics. Not only will doing this add rich color to your room, it will also give your walls a plush texture. Buy curtains and mount them to your walls either using curtain rods or even thumbtacks or nails. If curtains are too expensive, you can also use long bolts of fabric. Either way, make sure that they pleat; do *not* tack them on flat or your room will look like an inside-out birthday present.

Opt for deep or richly-hued fabrics: reds, purples, and golds. White is also a good choice. (Yes, haven't you heard? White can be Goth.)

In respect to what material to choose, velvet looks great but can get dusty; satin and cotton can be attractive as well.

VOLTAIRE • PHOTO: ODDREE

FLOOR IT!

If you already have a nice inlaid wood floor, consider yourself lucky. When I moved into my present apartment, the floors were covered with an atrocious white and blue linoleum floor that one would even hesitate to use in a kitchen. And it was everywhere! I hated it; but replacing a floor can be very expensive and seems like a pointless expense when you are renting.

Fortunately, though, you can easily hide such atrocities with throw rugs. Oriental rugs will lend your place a

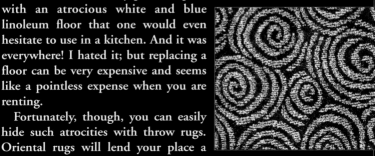

luxurious and opulent look. Solid black or red carpeting works nicely, too. But don't use a color that's the same as your walls, unless you *really* wish to go insane in short order! For example, if your walls are red, consider a black carpet. I was able to find at a local store a black carpet with sepia colored spirals; I affectionately call it the *Nightmare Before Christmas* rug. I was able to buy just a small remnant for very little money, as I am *blessed* with a tiny Manhattan apartment. I subsequently cut it myself to fit the space.

Additionally, throwing some black, purple, or red velvet cushions on the floor will add to the bohemian feel of your space ('cause face it, Goth is really just Hippie in black). And at the end of the day, your floor should be comfortable, because Goths tend to spend a lot of time on the floor (weeping, sulking, writing bad poetry, or just waiting for the madness to stop).

I'VE GOT YOU COVERED

So, you have ugly suburban furniture? Can't afford luxurious antique armchairs? Don't fret. Here's a really universal and affordable technique to turn it all into sumptuous gothic furniture. Step one: Get a large piece of fabric. Step two: Throw it over your couch and tuck it in. That's it!

Suddenly that ghastly, daisy-print sofa looks strangely spooky (1). Toss some lovely cushions on the seat and a lace shawl over the top for an extra touch of improvised Gothic-chic (2 & 3). Ugly end tables become elegant pedestals by simply shrouding them in lush black fabric. Top these surfaces with a skull, some candles, and other curios or mysterious bric-a-brac and no one will ever think to look underneath. You can do the same with just about any piece of furniture (except for the TV—covering it makes it *really* hard to watch).

All of the tables in my place are merely plastic

storage bins covered in black synthetic satin (1 & 2). They look great, and this way no one needs to know that I own thousands of dollars-worth of action figures. Though I will admit it's a major pain in the arse when I suddenly have a craving to play with my limited edition, Japanese repaint Edward Scissorhands doll with twenty-three points of articulation (adjusts glasses and reaches for asthma inhaler) (3)!

VOLTAIRE • PHOTO: ODDREE

PANE RELIEVERS

Nothing is more annoying than your pesky neighbors peering into your inner sanctum while you are sacrificing a goat. And when you're fast asleep (at 3 PM) you *really* don't need that big, yellow, hurty-thing (I think it's called the "sun") disturbing your exquisite, little piece of sweet sweet death. So when it comes to Gothic window treatments, the going logic is to block out as much light as you can. Do this with thick black velvet curtains. If you can't find black, go with another dark, rich color.

Also, these days it's quite easy to find ornate and elegant curtain rods—made of wood or wrought

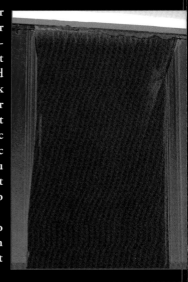

metal—without breaking the bank. But if you can't afford them, just nail the curtains directly to the window frame (hell, your tables are made out of milk crates, so what are you fussing about?).

LET THE GAMES BEGIN!

So now your walls are painted, your floor and windows are covered and your furniture seems to have disappeared under waves of black fabric. It's time to adorn your space with items that scream Goth!

Enter, if you dare, into the next few chapters for an assortment of Gothic how-to projects and discover the art of turning horridly mundane objects into fabulously macabre masterpieces!

gothic bottle candelabra

Light Up Your World with Darkness

NOTHING SAYS "GOTH" QUITE LIKE A SET OF CANDELABRA. WATCH ANY GOTHIC HORROR FILM AND YOU ARE BOUND TO SEE THEM IN THE BACKGROUND ILLUMINATING DARK CORNERS. THEY ARE ELEGANT and romantic—and if they have enough layers of wax cascading down the sides, they can be downright magnificent. I have a pair of them in my home that was inherited from a shoot I did for the Sci-Fi Channel a few years ago (a series of promos for the vampire show, *Forever Knight*). They were purchased at Pier One, look great, and if I recall correctly, weren't terribly expensive.

Not everyone, however, has an expense account to throw money around when it comes to buying candelabra. Years ago, when living in an apartment on the Lower East Side of Manhattan, I went for six years without electricity (by choice) (and was also, coincidentally, very low on funds). During that time, I stumbled upon a way to make beautiful candelabra by putting a spooky spin on an old, Italian restaurant staple.

It all started out of necessity: it was dark. I went downstairs to the bodega where—thanks to the Hispanic fascination with Santeria (something to which I was no stranger growing up)—there was an inexhaustible supply of candles between the Goya beans and the plantain chips. I bought some, stuck them in bottles for lack of anything else to stick them in, and voilà, there was light. And I saw that it was good.

But the real joy came weeks later when layers upon layers of wax had built up on the bottles and they took on an extremely romantic, old-world appearance. My then-girlfriend and I would sit there in the candlelight gazing at them. She said it looked like clouds, I said it looked like heaven.

Here's how to make them:

1) FIND SOME EMPTY BOTTLES. I will freely admit that I am a very big fan of any art project that starts out with emptying a bunch of bottles of wine . . . or port, or rum, or pretty much any other type of libation for that matter. If you are too young to drink, ask your parents to give the bottles to you. If they don't drink (then you are probably not living up to your job of being a really difficult teenager!), go to a local restaurant and ask them for their empty bottles. If they think you're weird or some kind of terrorist or something, just wait until recycling day and dig them out of their trash. Countless squatters will tell you that helping yourself to other people's garbage is *not* stealing.

2) PAINT IT BLACK! Well actually, if the bottles are beautiful and elaborate and have wonderfully old-fashioned labels reminiscent of a bygone era, you might choose to leave them as they are. But *please*—unless you are sporting a mullet and live below the Mason-Dixon line—do *not* make your candelabra out of bottles of Boone's Farm Wine! We're going for *Count Dracula* here, not *Dukes of Hazard*.

Either way, for a really Goth look, give the bottles a good misting of ultra flat black spray paint.

3) TIME TO DECORATE! Truth be told, the bottles will look just fine if they are all black. But for that extra touch of spooky elegance, feel free to decorate them with stickers of skulls, bats, or whatever gothic icons suit your fancy. For my candelabra, I printed out my own Gothy designs and affixed them to the bottles with spray adhesive. You can do the same with your own dark imagery or even pictures taken from books or magazines. Simply cut out the design, spray the back with spray adhesive, and attach to the bottle.

4) YOU CAN CHOOSE to keep the bottles separate (so that you can scatter them about your house); or if you prefer, glue the

1

2a

2b

3a

bottles together using a hot glue gun to create one big, massive candelabra of doom. Believe me when I say that you will be amazed at how much light they give off when clumped together.

5) **PICK YOUR CANDLES.** White candles look best. As they melt, they coat the bottles with streams of dripping wax and eventually develop into forms that look like they came straight from Dracula's castle. Do *NOT* buy "dripless" candles as this will defeat the whole purpose. Now light your candles, sit back, and relax! After a couple of weeks the wax will build up and give your candelabra that "I found it in the Phantom of the Opera's lair" look!

6) **IF YOU ARE IMPATIENT** like I am and just can't wait for the wax to build up, feel free to help it along. Hold a lit candle close to the top of a mounted candle; this will allow parts of it to trickle away and will make the drip formations look more dramatic.

VARIATIONS

There is no one right way to do this project. Add your own personal touch or use one of the variations below to make a candelabra that suits your specific taste.

Passion and Hate

For a sexier look, try red candles instead of white ones (though they do tend to look a tad satanic). You can also incorporate black candles, but that might be overdoing it and will most likely give your candelabra a very oppressive look. But then again, hey—maybe you get down like that.

The Band-elabra

Create your own "Band-elabra" by cutting out pictures of your favorite band and spray-mounting them to the bottles. "Hey look! It's The Cure (to darkness)!" Let Siouxsie Sioux light up your life. Or just sit and watch Peter Murphy wax poetic.

The Flik-er

Movies can also be a great source for a themed candelabra. Images from *The Nightmare Before Christmas* spray-mounted to the bottles will surely delight your friends. Other good choices include *The Crow*, *The Rocky Horror Picture Show*, *Dracula*, or just about anything by Tim Burton.

Don't worry about copyright issues if you are merely making one or two pieces for your home or for a gift. Just don't get crazy and start selling Darth Vader candelabra online or Lucas *will* send Boba Fett—*Esquire and Associates*—after you!

The Vampyre

If you look around a well-stocked liquor store, you may find a certain Transylvanian import called Vampire Wine. Yes, it's really imported from Transylvania! Packaged in a nice black bottle with a spooky label, these folks have done all of the work for you. Simply empty the bottles and stick candles in them. Voila! You have just taken your first step into the wonderful world of vampire lighting.

The Scandal-abra

Make a five-bottle candelabra (or use how ever many bottles apply to your respective situation), with each bottle featuring photos of your last few girlfriends or boyfriends. Make sure there is one extra bottle that you keep blank. Burn black candles—they are usually burned to wish people harm—and prominently place the apparatus in a very visible part of your home. Have a camera ready nearby.

When you bring a date to your house and he/she inquires about this odd contraption, explain that the photos are of your ex-lovers. When he/she asks you what the blank one is for, quickly take a picture of your date and say nothing.

Scandalous!

BURNIN' DOWN THE HOUSE!

Achtung! Needless to say, fire is dangerous. *Never* leave your candles lit while asleep or away from your home. Burning down your house and/or dying in a fire is not at all Goth (it's Punk!).

So, make sure you blow out those candles before returning to your coffin.

WHAT A DRIP!

Keep in mind that once this thing gets cookin', it's going to be a big, wonderfully drippy mess. And naturally the surface it's placed on is going to get covered in wax. So, make sure it's either a smooth surface (like glass) that can be cleaned, or an expendable surface (like a cheap, black satin tablecloth) that can be discarded if need be.

Alright. Now go make yourself a spooky bottle candelabra and light up your dark, dreary world in a way that won't make you seem the least bit cheery!

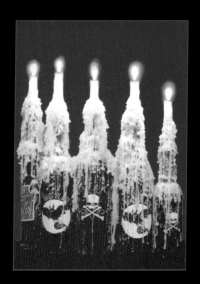

the grimoire

How to Turn a Plain Sketchbook into a Diabolical Book of the Dead

A LONG TIME AGO IN A GALAXY FAR, FAR AWAY (THAT IS, SOMETIME AROUND MARCH OF 1995 IN NEW YORK CITY'S EAST VILLAGE), I WAS ABOUT TO PLAY MY FIRST SHOW. I HAD BEEN TO MANY OTHER goth-rock shows prior to this and had noticed that bands would walk around before or after their performances carrying clipboards. The purpose of said clipboards was to collect the names and addresses of attendees to add to the band's mailing list; thusly, when the band would play another show, they could send invitations to people who might actually be interested in seeing them perform again. This is a smart practice for bands that wish to build a fan-base, and certainly for bands opposed to playing to an empty room.

While prepping for my premier performance, I realized that I should employ a similar means of collecting addresses; but—like with most things I observe—I couldn't help but to put my own spooky spin on it. It also occurred to me that people might be reticent to divulge their personal information without a good reason (and seeing a band's next performance might not be compelling enough for them to do it). Therefore, I set out to create a scenario that I felt would perhaps be more *encouraging* for those souls drawn to all things macabre.

I went to an art supply store and bought a plain sketchbook. I then spent a good deal of time altering it to make it appear like an ancient grimoire that I might have disinterred from Edgar Allen Poe's final resting place. While a grimoire is typically a manual for invoking spirits and demons, my grimoire would serve a different but equally nefarious purpose. The night of the show, somewhere in the middle

f my set, I stopped and held up this horrible, unholy-looking ledg—
nd proclaimed, "This is the Book of the Dead. If you put you—
ame and address in it, you will surely die!" (Long pause). I contin—
ed, "Not anytime soon, of course. But I can pretty much guarante—
ou that it will *eventually* happen." After the show most of the atten—
ees eagerly added their names and addresses (a good number i—
ather flashy and ostentatious handwriting) with a gold calligraph—
arker. And thus I stayed in touch with so many of the people wh—
ame to my early shows, and I was able to invite them to subsequer—
erformances. And to the best of my knowledge, few of them (if any—
ave since expired . . . but give it time! Muahahahahahahah!

To supplement my income, I also made scores of these grimoire—
r local stores. The Goth shops ate them up! As we all know, Goth—
ave a penchant for writing poetry during the wee hours of th—
orning in all-night cafes. And I can tell you from experience tha—
riting in a Mead spiral notebook just doesn't compare to bein—
ied scribbling in what looks like an unearthed tome from *Evi—
ead*. To the observer, your pathetic, pretentious drivel about bat—
ring out of bell towers or your heart being as black as the moonles—
ght takes on the appearance of a potentially potent spell that wil—
ondemn the souls of all who look upon the verses.

When people would approach me and ask about the Book of the—
ead, I would look at them and flatly say, "I found it in a grave."—
nd the poor, wide-eyed fools would believe me! Little did the—
ow how easy it was to make.

To concoct your own ghastly grimoire sketchbook, follow these—
mple instructions:

In order to demonstrate a couple of styles from
which you can choose, I decided to make two
sketchbooks; we will call one the Medieval
Grimoire and the other the Gothic Grimoire.
Regardless of which you opt to create, the first
step is simple: buy a plain, hardcover sketchbook
from your local art supply store. Try to find one
with a black cover. If you can procure one with

Either way, avoid getting a book with lined pages (unless you want your book to look like the Accursed Grimoire of Proper Penmanship 101).

2) Gather some items with which to decorate your book.

For the Medieval Grimoire (a) I went to a hardware store and purchased some drawer handles and brass hinges. If you can find a nice, old-fashioned-looking lock, that will add a nice touch as well.

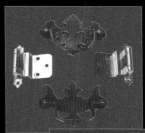

For the Gothic Grimoire (b) I gathered some small plaster skulls I had made a few years ago, a rubber bat from a novelty store, and a piece of jewelry (specifically, a cross formed from horseshoe nails I picked up while in Toronto, but just about any piece of Gothic jewelry will do).

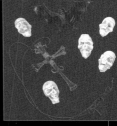

3) Glue your chosen items onto your sketchbook using a hot glue gun. Don't worry if it's a bit messy—this will only further establish that desired wretched and weathered appearance.

4) Once all of the items are attached, stand the book upright and drip hot glue onto the cover. Use gravity to artfully direct your drips. This will create the illusion that the glue is actually age-old candle wax. (Everyone knows that all of the ancient necromancers wrote their best spells by candlelight. Logic dictates that some candles were bound to get knocked over, dribbling wax onto their books—

especially with all of those pesky demons flying about!)

5) Once the glue is dry, paint the front of the book black. Use acrylic paint and a brush to get into all of the cracks. Don't use spray paint or else you will end up inadvertently coloring the edges of the pages too!

6) If you wish, you can leave your book solid black. It will look pretty fabulous as is. If you end here, spray Crystal Clear or some other spray shellac to seal the paint. And you are done!

7) I like to add some extra dimension by dry-sponging a lighter color over the black. (Photographers like to overuse the term "painting with light;" I like to call this technique "lighting with paint.") Mix up a small batch of gray paint using white and black acrylics (I added a touch of silver paint as well to create the slight effect of a metallic patina). Dab a sponge in the paint and then tap it several times on a piece of newspaper until the sponge is almost dry. Then, pat the sponge lightly all over the surface of your book. The gray paint will tint only the raised areas and will not get into the cracks and crevices, making it seem as though light were just grazing the

surface of the cover. This will instill the book with a more timeworn appearance and will highlight its three-dimensionality.

8) You now have a gorgeous grimoire (or two) in which to write your pernicious poems or draw your dastardly doodles.

9) To *really* bat your grimoire out of the Gothic park, you will need to paint the pages. Be warned: this is a time consuming and tedious process, and requires access to a fireplace. But if you are serious about going for an ancient, exhumed look, this is how to get it: Squirt some sepia paint into a small bowl of water so that you have a mixture that, when applied to a piece of scrap paper, tints the paper but does not leave an opaque coat. Once you have achieved the appropriate translucence, paint the first page with a large house painting brush. Turn the page and do the next one. Continue through the whole book this way (yes, I warned you that it would be tedious). Be very careful, as the wet pages may be prone to tearing.

After painting every page, sit the book in front of a fireplace for a day or two (I told you this was hardcore!). The heat from the fire will dry the pages and as they dry, they will become wonderfully warped. You will be amazed by the results! Your one-inch-thick sketchbook will expand to many times its original thickness (due to the pages deforming). And with that creepy cover you crafted, no one will be able to doubt you when you proclaim that you found it in a graveyard under the bones of a long-dead warlock!

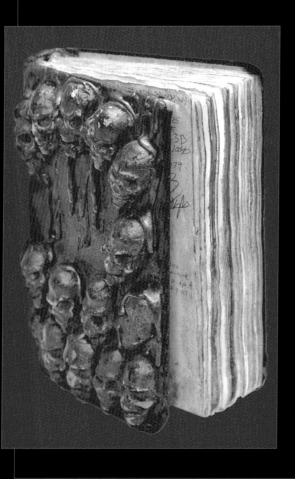

gothic baby doll

Tinkering with Terrible Toys

IF YOU WALK INTO ANY COMIC BOOK STORE
THESE DAYS YOU ARE BOUND TO FIND A HORDE OF
PIERCING GOTHIC EYES STARING BACK AT YOU. NO,
NOT FROM LENORE FANS, SILLY! I MEAN FROM A
extensive array of gothic dolls. The Living Dead Dolls by Mezco
paved the road a few years ago and proved with their popularity that
the world was ready for spooky toys. Consequently, as of late it has
seemed like a lot of folks have been jumping on the Gothic doll
bandwagon.

Once upon a time, though, when it was unthinkable for any company to make such a thing, it was far more likely that the only way
to possess a doll as wonderfully spooky as yourself was to make one.
Throughout the '80s and '90s my friends and I would make them for
fun; now we are all tired, old Goths and just let manufacturers do all
of the work. Nevertheless, the dark secrets of turning wretched, little baby dolls into denizens of the Batcave abide in my sinister cere-
brum. I will *never* divulge the formula! *Never*!

Oh, okay. You talked me into it. But
just this one time.

Follow these steps (adding your own
touches and flair along the way) to make
a dreadful little Goth doll of your own:

) I went down to Chinatown and
bought this generic baby doll. Isn't
it hideous?! In no time it will
become *wonderfully* hideous. Just
you watch.

If your doll has nice eyes, cover them with a piece of tape. You don't want to end up painting the eyes white . . . unless you are making a Marilyn Manson doll!

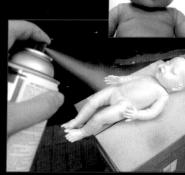

A doll with a rosy complexion is simply not going to do! Take your doll outside and spray paint it white. For a more realistic effect, give the face a nice opaque coat, but only mist the rest of the body. That will make the face look paler than the body, which will have flesh undertones showing through.

Afterwards, be sure to let the paint dry for a few hours (or even overnight); otherwise, it may be difficult to draw over it with marker, which is what comes next.

Now it's time to do what Goths do best: apply makeup! With a brush and some acrylic paint—choose a nice Gothy color like crimson, magenta, or a deep purple— paint in the eye shadow. Add black lipstick and elaborate eyebrow designs.

If you are not that deft at painting with a brush you can add some of the finer details with a magic marker.

6) Create the Gothic makeup of your dreams (or is that nightmares?).

7) I like to spray Workable Fixative over the face to seal the makeup.

A word of caution, though: some spray sealants or clear glazes dissolve marker! So, go easy on the spraying or your doll's makeup will drip and run and look like . . . well, like yours at the end of a night of clubbing!

8) Wardrobe time! Buy a pair of fishnet stockings (or fish one out of the hamper for that "What's that smell? Patchouli?" effect). With a pair of scissors, snip off the tip where one's toes would go; then, move the scissors up the leg of the stocking about four inches and cut again. Now you should have a tube made of fishnet stocking.

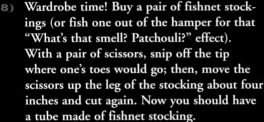

9) Slip the fishnet tube over your doll's head and let it rest around its torso.

If you are a Goth worth your weight in cloves, you have pulled many a pair of fishnet stockings over your own head before. This is no different, just on a smaller scale.

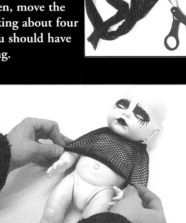

10) Make an incision in the stockings about one inch down from the doll's shoulder and slip the arm through it. Do the same for the other arm. Now you have a fishnet tank top.

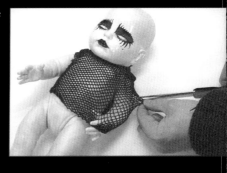

Oh, if it were only this easy to make a top *you* could wear!

11) Now it's time to whip up an insta-fetish style with some faux-vinyl gauntlets and leggings. It's remarkably easy to pull off!

Just get a roll of black electrical tape and wrap it around the arms and legs. Electrical tape is somewhat elastic, so the tighter you pull it, the better it will conform to your doll's anatomy. And vinyl—even fake vinyl on a doll—should be nothing if not skin-tight.

12) Has anybody ever told you that your clothes were so tight that they looked painted on? Well, I find painting the baby doll's thong to be a whole lot easier than trying to tailor one to fit its little body (it also makes me feel a hell of a lot less creepy).

I used a brush and acrylic paint to create the panties, but you can use a marker if you prefer.

13) Store-bought temporary tattoos can really go a long way in decorating your doll. I picked up some skull and spider designs for mine.

Apply them to your doll the same way as you would to yourself.

14) Spray your doll's tattoos with Workable Fixative, Crystal Clear, or any other kind of spray-sealant or shellac. This will help prevent the tattoos from peeling or flaking off.

15) Unless your doll is going to be sporting the "Fester," you will need to add hair. A piece of black fake fur works well. Just cut out a piece big enough for the top of the head, glue it to the doll with a glue gun, and style just as you'd coif your own.

16) I decided to give my doll a Mohawk for a more old-school Deathrocker look. I cut a strip of fur from the rim of a fur hat and glued it to the doll's head. Oi!

17) If you plan to include any, draw in the sideburns, stubble, bangs, and or whatever other hair details with a marker.

18) Don't forget to cover the finger-nails and toenails with some obligatory black nail polish.

19) With the doll just about finished, I decided to take it to Saint Mark's Place for a little jewelry shopping! What's a Goth doll without a little bit of Gothic bling-bling, yo?

20) Choose some Gothy jewelry for your doll. Mine made off with an ankh necklace (a), a cross earring (b), and a nose ring (c). It must be Christmas!

VOLTAIRE • PHOTO: ODDREE

21) Pierce the nose and ear(s) with a heavy sewing needle. Then, secure the jewelry in place with some crazy glue.

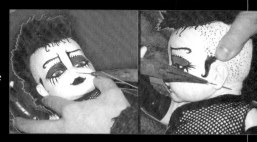

22) Skirts are easy to make! Just find yourself a cool Gothy sock—maybe a Halloween sock with jack-o-lanterns or skulls on it. Cut off a tube-shaped piece from above the ankle portion and there you have it—a spooky skirt for your Gothic dolly.

Personally, I prefer my Gothic dolls in little more than a thong; therefore, I passed on the skirt.

And behold! In only a few hours, my little Gothic Deathrocker doll is complete!

43

LIVING DEAD DOLLS: READY-MADE AND READY TO ROCK

Of course, if all of this seems like a big hassle to you, just pick up a Living Dead Doll instead. Their creators, Damien Glonek and Ed Long, started out by making their own dolls using techniques not

PHOTO: MEZCO TOYS

dissimilar to those described in this section. A few years ago, Mezco Toys caught wind of them and provided the means for them to spread their spookiness across the lands. They have countless designs from which to choose and they are all pretty damn cool!

A *TRULY LIVING* UNDEAD DOLL:

I was playing at a sci-fi/horror convention a year or so ago when a couple of Goths (Frank and Gwen) approached me holding a pair of homemade Gothic dolls. They had painted their faces with Gothic makeup and dressed them in black gowns. I was delighted to see that there were still Goths out there making their own toys. They held these two diminutive Gothlings before me, when a terrifying thing

happened! As if possessed, the dolls opened their eyes, mumbled some garbled incantation, and started moving their mouths in a bizarre sucking motion! To say the very least, it was extremely disconcerting (and yet kind of alluring). I then learned that Frank and Gwen make their customized Goth dolls using store-bought dolls that have mechanized facial expressions and recorded voices.

So, if you want to give your doll that extra psychotic touch, follow their demented lead and find yourself a manufactured doll that *really* sucks.

Oh, you know what I mean!

GWEN • PHOTO: FRANK

the goth box

A New Spin on Spooky Shelving

HERE'S A LITTLE TRICK I PICKED UP WHILE LIVING ON THE LOWER EAST SIDE OF MANHATTAN.
BEING A STOP-MOTION ANIMATOR, I HAD TONS OF RUBBER MODELS OF SKELETONS, MONSTERS, dragons, etc, and nowhere in my flat to really display them. And putting up shelving is right up there on my list of the most annoying ways to spend an afternoon (especially when the walls of your tenement apartment are cracked, distressed, and far from flat). As I've mentioned, New Yorkers are notorious for throwing away perfectly good stuff and I took advantage of that phenomenon to furnish my entire apartment. And so, one day while walking down the street keeping an eye out for discarded furniture I found an old armoire. It was in terrible shape, but something possessed me to pull out one of the drawers. I held it up and suddenly realized that if I were to nail it to a wall, it would make a great display case! I took it home, nailed it to the wall, and put one of my animation models in it. Lo and behold, I was right! Not only was installing it much easier than putting up shelving, but it framed whatever was put inside in such a way as to make its contents look like very special works of art.

From that point on I kept an eye out for discarded dressers that I could pillage for their drawers. Eventually, I had dozens of them on my walls (some square, some rectangular, and some from baroque-style armoires, which had beautifully arched shapes) and all of my little monsters were wonderfully exhibited as if in a gallery.

I call this contraption a Goth Box (hey, isn't that a compilation of Goth music put out by Cleopatra?). My name for it aside, this is actually a technique that could work in anyone's home, Goth or not—just plain wooden drawers themselves, with no painting or other alterations, work as well as decorated ones. Simply nail them to the wall and you are done.

Still, I like mine black and red for an elegant Japanese/Goth look. Follow these easy steps to create a similar Goth Box of your very own:

1) First you will need to find one or more dresser or chest drawers. I've had great success finding them abandoned on the street, but if your neighborhood doesn't really offer such possibilities, you can still get a good deal on an old dresser at a flea market or Salvation Army store.

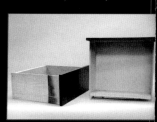

2) Paint the outside of the drawer black. I used acrylic paint. Enamel, latex, or any kind of house paint will also work well. This time, though, avoid using spray paint as it tends to not look so good when used on wood.

3) In a cup, dilute some red paint with water (I used an acrylic paint in a crimson hue). The idea is to brush this watery mixture on the inside of the drawer to stain the wood, as opposed to painting it with an opaque layer. Depending on how watery your paint is, it might take more than one application. A couple of coats of watered-down crimson paint will give a wonderfully rich, blood-soaked appearance to the wood while still preserving the visibility of the natural grain.

4) There you have it! Nail it to a wall and you have a beautiful Goth Box in which to display your favorite skull, doll, or other Gothic curio.

gothic picture frames

Turning Boring Frames into Frightful Borders

ADORNING YOUR WALLS WITH ART IS AN EXCELLENT WAY TO GIVE A DRAB ROOM A DREADFULLY OPULENT TOUCH. AND A TRIP TO A HIGH-END FRAME SHOP WILL UNDOUBTEDLY PRESENT YOU with myriad elaborate frames for your artwork. Chances are, though, the scariest part of them will be the price.

Fortunately, with some easy-to-find, inexpensive frames and some household objects you can create elegantly freaky frames of your own that are worthy of the Gothic art you will display within them. Most importantly, they won't put a grave-sized hole in your wallet!

In this section, I will demonstrate how to make three different designs; we will call them the Hell Raiser, the Glue Gun Baroque, and the Classic Gothic frames. While they all share a dark aesthetic, the styles are different enough to match various tastes. Choose the one that is right for you, or make them all!

1) The first step was the same for all of the designs—a trip to Wholesale Liquidators, where I purchased three inexpensive picture frames (ranging in price from $5 to $10). I rolled up my sleeves, removed the backing and the glass from each, and got to work.

2) To make the Hell Raiser frame, get yourself a handful of wood screws. With a drill (I used a cordless one to save me from a sore wrist!), drive the screws into the wood in a random pattern and at different angles. Be careful not to place the screws too close together as doing so could split the wood.

3) When you have finished driving in the screws, your frame will have a wonderfully tortured look to it.

4) Take the frame outside and spray paint it black (I used glossy black to give it a nice sheen).

5) Once the spray paint has thoroughly dried, mix up some red paint. I used acrylic paint, but just about any kind will do (enamel, house paint, etc.). Choose a nice rich color like crimson or scarlet. Dip a brush into the paint. Hold the brush several inches above the frame and flick the brush back and forth to create splatters of red. The resulting effect will look like a ghoulishly gory spray of blood. Once done, let the red paint dry. If you desire, you can spray on a coat of Crystal Clear or some other shellac to seal it and give the whole frame a shiny finish.

6) There you have it—a frightful frame in which to enclose a photo of the dolorous demon of your dreams!

THE GLUE GUN BAROQUE FRAME

"Glue gun baroque," as I like to call it, is a technique I came up with in the late '80s/early '90s while working in the stop-motion and prop departments of an animation company. You will be amazed at how elaborate and elegant you can make an item look using little more than hot glue and some paint.

1) First, lay your picture frame down on a flat, protected surface. Plug in a glue gun; once it has heated up, hold it above the surface of your frame and let the hot glue drip down onto it. Gently move your wrist about in random circular patterns and watch as the glue creates odd and intricate designs on the wood.

   A hint: The closer you hold the glue gun to the wood, the thicker the drizzles of glue will be. Hold the glue gun higher up to get really tiny, intricate patterns. You may want to experiment with this technique on a piece of cardboard or newspaper before doing it on your frame.

2) Once the glue has dried, you have what might appear to be patterns sculpted onto your frame. But don't stop here— because, truth be told, it still just looks like a bunch of hot glue squirted onto some wood.

3) Take your frame outside and coat it with ultra flat black spray paint.

4) Now that the whole frame is black, the glue patterns *really* appear to be part of the frame, rather than something that was added on.

5) In order to make the patterns stand out even more, mix up some acrylic paint and apply it using a dry-sponge technique. Gray works well, but to get a metallic effect, use gold, copper, or bronze acrylic paint. Dab a sponge in the paint, pat it on a newspaper until there is hardly any wet paint left on it, and then tap the sponge lightly all over the frame. The extruded surface areas (i.e., the dribbles of glue) will get a touch of color and the recessed areas (i.e., the black wooden part) will remain black, giving your frame the look of corroded metal.

6) Your guests will swear that you own an expensive and intricately carved work of art. Just don't tell them that all it took was about $20 in supplies and an hour of your time!

This design employs a technique that I frequently use to make mundane objects appear to be ancient, decrepit works of Gothic art (see the section on making a grimoire). With a variety of macabre found objects, hot glue, and some paint, you can make just about any item seem like it was unearthed from the catacombs of a medieval cathedral!

1) First, select a frame that has a wide border; you will need the space in order to glue your items to it (a narrow one—like that used for the Hell Raiser frame—will not be able to accommodate your spooky decorations).

2) Collect an array of objects with which you will adorn your frame. I chose a couple of real skulls (a beaver skull and a fox skull I bought at a natural science store in Manhattan), some smaller human skulls (hand-sculpted out of Super Sculpy), some rubber lizards (purchased from a gum ball machine at 25¢ each), and some little longhorn skulls (harvested from a Mardi Gras necklace I bought in New Orleans during Goth Con 2!).

3) Place all of your items on your frame to get a sense of where they will look best. Rearrange them until you come up with an acceptable design.

4) Using a glue gun, attach your items to the frame.

5) Once again, it's time for my patented drippy technique. (I should seriously trademark this! Maybe I'll call it, "Voltaire-ifying" an object . . . then again, maybe not.) As seen in the section on how to make a grimoire, stand your picture frame upright and drip hot glue on it, creating what seem to be oozing streams of old candle wax.

6) At this point, your project will look like a picture frame with a lot of creepy chachkas glued to it—not a very impressive thing to look at.

7) Take it outside and coat it with ultra flat black spray paint. I never cease to be amazed by the power of painting something black! All of a sudden, the frame begins to actually look like something menacing!

8) Whip up some gray acrylic paint and dry-sponge it on the frame. This will really make the skulls and other objects come to life!

9) Voilà! You have created a Gothic picture frame sure to chill your friends to the marrow!

There you have it! All three frames were created over the course of a couple of hours and at very little expense. Regardless, they make whatever you display inside them seem like truly special works of art.

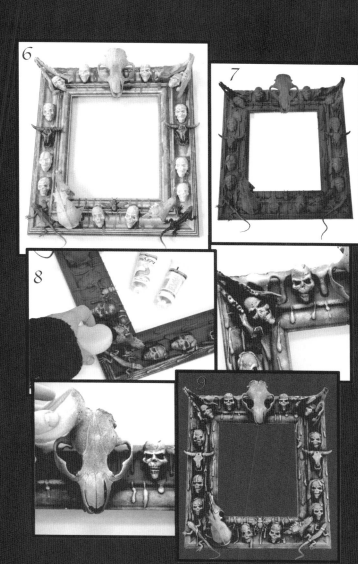

gothic flower arranging

Decorating with Dead Things

THEY SAY THAT CHILDREN SHOULDN'T PLAY WITH DEAD THINGS. I SAY, "PSHAW!" Goth is all about death! Okay, not really. It's mostly about stuff that looks cool when it's dead (and the subsequent writing of crappy poems thereof). Naturally then, when it comes to decorating with flowers, you will most likely find yourself using ones that have shuffled off this mortal coil (do flowers have a mortal coil? Hmm . . . I feel a poem coming on). It seems that most people are prone to discarding their bouquets the moment the slightest sign of wilting occurs as they no longer find them appealing (foolish mortals!). Don't they know how easy it is to dry flowers? In so doing, you lock in their natural splendor, preserving their beauty for years to come. Bouquets of desiccated roses make for wonderful trimming and will give your den an air of romance and old-world charm.

Follow these simple steps to create your own bouquets of decayed blossoms:

1) Get your hands on a few dozen roses. If you happen across some freshly discarded ones, these will work just fine. If you are buying them, feel free to get the cheapest available; there's no point in spending a mint on flowers that you plan to kill.

2) Hammer one or more nails into your wall.

3) Wrap a rubber band around the stems of each bouquet and hang them upside down.

4) In about a week your flowers will be dry and because they were hung upside down, will retain their beautiful shape. Turn them right side up and place them in vases around your place or if you prefer, leave them where they are as wall decorations.

Here are some suggested variations:

Black Roses

A great alternative—and a true scene staple—is the artificial black rose. You can find them at silk flower stores or on the Internet. They can be used to decorate not only your interior, but your hair and your clothes as well. In short, they will add a decidedly Gothic flair to anything you use them on. Personally though, I prefer dried plants in my decorating endeavors; depending on where you live, though, they may be difficult to come by.

LILAH • PHOTO: NADYA LEV

The Dried Flower Shop

Using decayed foliage and flora for decoration does not need to end at dried roses. If you are lucky enough to have a dried and/or artificial flower shop near you, you have access to an extensive selection of desiccated plants, weeds, and pods that can look very creepy, if not downright extraterrestrial in origin. I often frequent the dried flower district in my hometown of Manhattan (yes, we have an entire district!) where I am surrounded by all manner of dried plants, artificial vines, silk flowers, etc. With so much from which to choose, it takes me a while to select my freaky favorites to use in decorating my dreadful domicile.

For those of you who don't have such a shop nearby, you will have to improvise. If you live in rural America (my condolences), you may be able to find some truly unique flowers, grains, twigs, and weeds growing wildly that you can harvest and dry yourself. And of course, barring that, the Internet also serves as a convenient source for procuring all of these items.

Black Branches

Here is an easy-to-make arrangement that will give your place a touch of "barren forest" chic:

1) Pick up some branches either gathered from outside or bought at a shop. Take the branches outside and spray-paint them black.

2) Once dry, tie the branches together with a piece of ribbon. Any ribbon will do; but something along the lines of a Halloween ribbon with a spider web pattern adds a nice touch.

3) Hammer a nail into the wall and use it to mount your branches.

4) The spindly, black branches give an interesting, organic touch to a flat red wall.

1) A good, grim bouquet requires dried greenery that is inherently spooky-looking; elements that fit the bill are pretty easy to come by at a dried flower store.

   The pieces that I selected were: (a) Curly willow branches for their wonderfully winding forms; (b) Some threateningly thorny thistle; (c) Clusters of Japanese lanterns for their exquisitely extraterrestrial shape (the pods look like something out of *Attack of the Body Snatchers!*); (d) Poppy pods for much the same reason; (e) Some pre-dyed red reeds of grain for dimension; (f) Some sparkling spider web decorations for that decidedly Gothic touch (these were store-bought; however, you could easily make your own with some twigs, hot glue, black paint, and glitter).

2) The willow was to serve as the backbone of the bouquet; therefore, I naturally started with that. I took it outside and coated it with glossy black spray paint.

3) I decided that the color scheme for the bouquet would be a Gothy black and red with silver accents. And so, while outside, I also spray-painted the poppy pods black and the thistle red.

4) In order to highlight the unusual shape of the poppy pods, I dry-sponged them with silver acrylic paint.

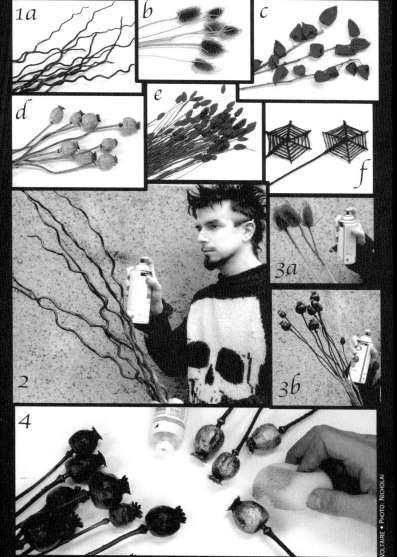

5) The Japanese lantern already had striking, reddish-orange pods. However, the green stems really clashed with the color-scheme (green is so *totally* un-Goth!). I therefore had my trusty assistant, Nicholai, paint the stems black with acrylic paint.

6) With all of the elements colored appropriately, it was time to assemble them into an arrangement. I first placed the willow branches flat on a table and spread them out in a fan shape. Then I placed a handful of the red stalks of grain in the center.

7) Using a tall vase as my base, I transferred the skeletal cluster. The ample stalks of grain in the center gave some body to the bouquet and the spiraling willow branches fanned out like the legs of a big sinister spider.

8) From that point on, it was just a matter of distributing the other plants in a circular pattern, thus filling out the rest of the bouquet.

When putting your arrangement together, it's important to consider the heights of the different items so that they can be clearly seen and appreciated; otherwise, your bouquet will just end up looking like a tangled jumble of bizarre shapes. I clipped the stems of the different plants so that they would sit at different levels in the bouquet. The curly willow extended the highest, followed by the poppy pods and thistle; below that were the stalks of grain, and finally, floating at the base of the arrangement, just above the rim of the vase, were the clusters of Japanese lanterns.

9) To match the spider-like look of the willow, I added a spider web decoration to the mix.

10) Behold—my completed Gothic bouquet!

Placed in a prominent spot in your spooky domicile, a similar Gothic bouquet is sure to capture the eye of your guests; and most impor-tantly, it's an excellent alternative to a gaudy, colorful arrangement of those icky *living* flowers!

5

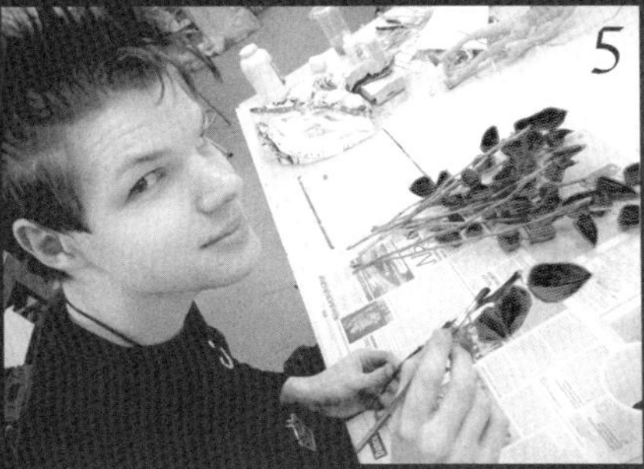

6

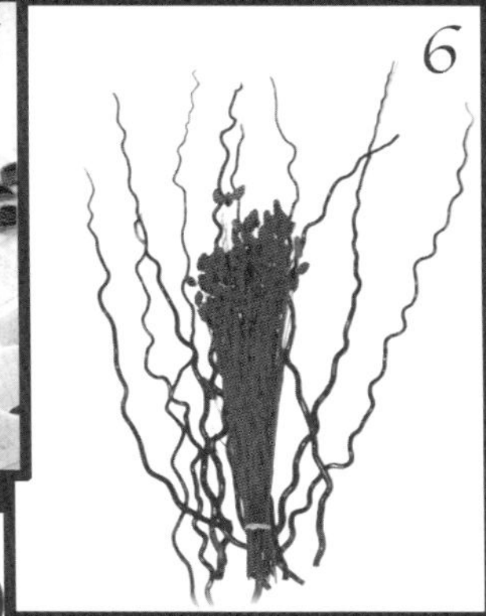

7

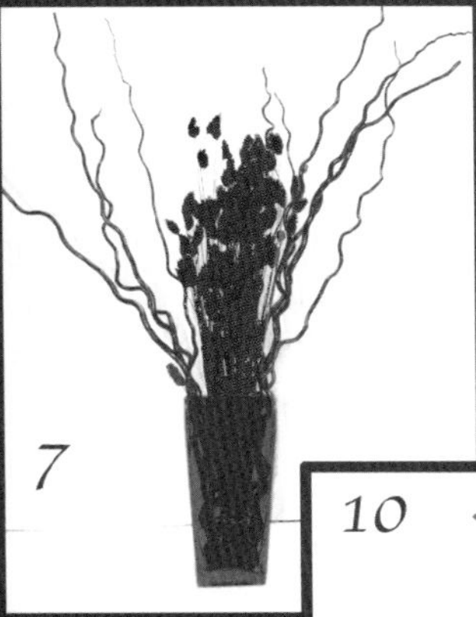

8

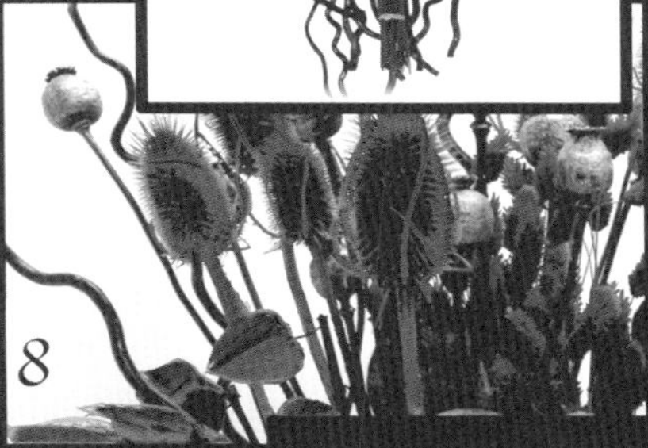

9

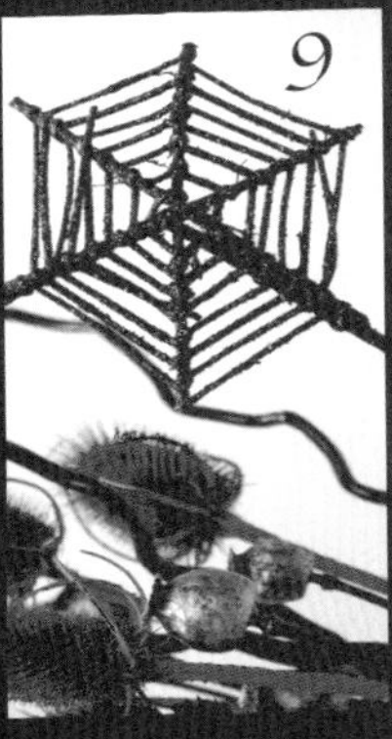

10

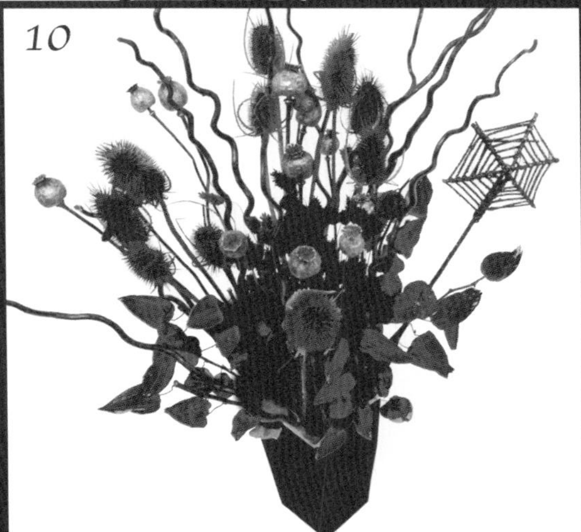

NICHOLAI • PHOTO: VOLTAIRE

graveyard cake

Have Your Grave and Eat It Too!

Contrary to popular belief, Goths love to celebrate. Hell, just about any occasion that allows for dining, dancing, and dressing up seems like a good enough reason to indulge in some merrymaking (or ennui-making, if you prefer). However, such festivities often require the presence of a cake and unless it's

Halloween time, you just know it's going to be impossible to find one that doesn't look like it was made for your little sister's sweet-sixteen party. And sure, a dense chocolate mud cake *might* look black in a dark enough Goth club. But does it really scream, "Spooky!"?

Belle Marie Antoinette said, "Let them eat cake!" and I couldn't agree more. So, I set out to concoct a confection that even a Goth wouldn't mind getting a bit of on their velvet cape. It had to be macabre, it had to be delicious, and it had to be easy to make (since most of us aren't professional pastry chefs). I enlisted the help of the

lovely Oddree, who baked while I took pictures and got very, very excited . . . um, about cake! Together we constructed an edible cemetery sure to delight your fiendish friends (and scare the crap out of everyone else).

It doesn't take a mad scientist to make my gruesome graveyard cake, just a couple of hours, some easily obtained supplies, and a love for the whimsically macabre.

Here's what you will need:

FOR THE CAKE:

2 boxes of chocolate fudge cake mix (I used a Duncan Hines mix but you can use whatever brand strikes your fancy. Check the back of the box to see what other ingredients you will need—eggs, oil, etc. Just remember that you will be making two cakes, so double up on the mix ingredients!)

Two 9 x 13 inch baking pans

FOR THE DECORATION:

1 tub of white vanilla frosting

One 1 oz. bottle of red food coloring

1 jar of cherry preserves (or whatever other jam you prefer; just make sure it's red, though.)

Red gummy worms

An assortment of cookies

1 tube of black decorative icing

A handful of twigs

1 can of black spray paint (yes, we are making a cake!)

1 spooky action figure

1 candle

1) Prepare all of the ingredients you will need for the cakes (read the back of the box for a list of the needed supplies. Again, remember that you will need twice as much of everything as you will be baking two cakes!).

1 A) Guys, if you don't bake (or even if you do), try to get a beautiful woman to bake the cake for you. I can't begin to tell you how much more fun it is this way!

2) Preheat the oven to the temperature indicated on the cake-mix box. While it warms up, add all the prescribed cake ingredients in a big bowl.

3) Thoroughly combine the ingredients using an electric mixer.

4) Evenly pour your cake mix into the two well-greased cake pans and throw them into the oven. Set a timer for the correct cooking time. Halfway through the total bake time, turn the pans around so that the cakes rise evenly. When they are done, set them aside and let them cool.

5) If you have baby bats fluttering about your place, hand over the bowl, spatula, or beaters. They'll love you for it!

1

1a

2

3

4

5

I'm so dark I fart BATS

6) Next, empty the whole tub of white vanilla frosting into a mixing bowl.

7) Add the entire bottle of red food coloring—we found that it took all of it to get the shade of red we desired.

8A) Using an electric mixer, blend the frosting and coloring until it is a uniform shade.

8B) If you have a camera, don't forget to take the obligatory shot of the hot girl licking frosting off the beaters (I took about fifty of them!)

9) Back to the cakes. These are going to serve as the muddy foundation of soil on which your graveyard is built; therefore, they will need to look accordingly. After removing them from the pans, cut off a half-inch strip all the way around the perimeter of each cake with a very sharp knife. The idea is to give the sides of the cakes a porous, earthy appearance.

10) Spread the cherry preserves on top of one of the cakes (you can also use strawberry, raspberry, or a different flavor if you like, but again, try to stick with something red). Then place the second cake on top of it, thus forming a two-layer cake.

11A) It's time to decorate your cake. This is where the fun really begins! Spread that decadent red icing onto the top of your cake.

11B) Do *not* apply icing to the sides! In order to make this look like a dug-up clump of earth, the porous sides of the cake should be left exposed.

12) Now for the spooky forest! Get a handful of twigs and spray paint them black. You can purchase some from a dried flower shop, or you can just collect them from outside.

13) Some people apparently have a weird and crazy aversion to having spray-painted items stuck into their food (the neurotic kooks!). If you also feel that getting poisoned while eating cake isn't your cup of tea, leave about an inch and a half of the twig bases unpainted. Or you can drip some wax from a candle onto the bases of your black twigs. This will keep the chemicals in the paint from seeping into your graveyard cake.

14) Stick the twigs into your cake to create a spooky forest.

15) What's a dark forest without some creepy night crawlers? Whip out those red gummy worms.

16) With a pair of scissors, cut them in half. Don't worry—this is far less gross than doing it with the real thing.

17) Stick the gummy worms between the two layers of cake. They should poke out in such a way that they appear to be crawling out of your graveyard.

18) A cemetery just isn't a cemetery without gravestones! Lay out a selection of cookies from the local supermarket. Try to find cookies with shapes reminiscent of gravestones: ladyfingers, Chessmen, or Social Tea Biscuits will do the job nicely.

19) Write on the cookies with the black decorative icing (you may need to buy a special nozzle to get the icing fine enough). Skulls, crosses, plenty of R.I.P.s will help to get the point across.

20) With your grim cookie gravestones decorated, simply stick them into the cake and arrange them to create a scene that looks like an old, abandoned cemetery.

21) And now for the finishing touch: choose a creepy action figure from your collection and place it atop your cadaverous cake. I chose a mini Living Dead doll for mine.

There you have it! It's spooky! It's creepy! It's . . . well, *delicious!* Best of all, it's easy to make (and even easier to eat!). In just a couple of hours and with very little baking skills, you have made a ghastly graveyard cake that will turn heads—even the severed ones!

pimp your ride, Dracula style

From Drab to "Dragula"

IT'S A DARK SATURDAY NIGHT. YOU'RE STANDING OUTSIDE OF THE OOKY-SPOOKY GOTH CLUB OF DOOM, BEDECKED IN YOUR VAMPIRIC FINERY. AS THE CLUB CLOSES, WAVES OF FRAZZLED GOTHS pour out onto the street. An argument ensues. Apparently Mistress Secretia, Defiler of the Clergymen, believes her haughty self to be Gother than thou! Heated words are exchanged. In your incensed state, you accidentally drop your driver's license. She swoops to the ground like a bat diving down upon its prey, picks the card up and proclaims your birth name for all to hear! The horror! The shame! A macabre melee breaks out—fangs go flying, capes are torn (hell hath no fury like a vampire scorned), wigs are pulled, top hats are crushed by pointy boots in a rush! You lunge. The crowd shrieks and protects its eyes from the burst of shrapnel (bits of custom fangs and black Lee Press-On Nails).

And then the victor arises. You stand triumphantly above the bruised body of your fallen foe with *her* driver's license in your hand. Bowed in the fecal position (no, that's not a typo) on the cold gray pavement, she winces as you announce, "Mistress Secretia, Defiler of the Clergymen is actually . . ." A sea of onlookers, fang-adorned mouths flung agape, hang on your every word. You continue, savoring every syllable: " . . . Tiffany Mandelbaum!"

There is a wave of laughter. A guy who looks like Uncle Fester swallows one of his fake fangs. Over the sounds of his choking, you pronounce your ominous victory speech to a crowd of captivated Gothlings. "Be thee warned, you children of the night—for I am no mere mortal! I am truly the darkest amongst thee. Dare not to defy me, lest I should choose to descend from my dark tower of superiority to wrestle thee to the ground, take *thine* driver's license and read *thine* birth name aloud for all to mock! Know now that I am and forever shall be the Gothest soul in all of (insert the name of your crappy town here)."

There is silence as the audience takes in your hallowed words.

"And now, I am off and away to my lair!"

And that's when you hop into your lavender Honda Accord and zip away into the shadows.

Okay. What's wrong with this picture? Well, alright. *Everything.*

But seriously, would it kill you to have a vehicle to jump into that's at least *half* as pompous as you are?

Time and time again, all of the flamboyance and pomp and circumstance of a Goth's life gets instantly flushed down the toilet the second they pull up in their car. If you are Goth *and* you drive, consider getting some wheels that fit the rest of your dramatic lifestyle.

Everyone knows that the single Gothest ride in town has got to be the hearse. Truly, when it comes to transportation, this is the ultimate way to declare, "I am *spooky* and there's nothing you can do about it!" You just can't get any Gother than riding around in a car created to haul corpses. They are not that hard to get your claws on and can be rather affordable if bought used. I know a handful of Goth and Psychobilly folks who own them and drive them with pure pride. But believe me, if you drive around in a hearse, you *will* get funny looks—especially when dropping off the baby bats at soccer practice. So, just keep in mind that a hearse is as much of a commitment as it is a statement.

Short of buying a hearse, you can at least try to not buy the goofiest car on the lot. Start by getting a car that's black—like I always say, if it's black, you're half way there. And there are other little things you can do to your car as well to Goth it up a bit; for example, putting Goth band stickers or spooky, anti-social bumper stickers on it—you know, ones with phrases like, "You laugh at me because I'm different. I laugh at you because you're all the same."

Truth be told, I always thought it would be exorbitantly expensive to *really* Goth-out your car—that is, until I saw my friend Asia

DeVinyl's car! By simply making some smart choices and spending a little bit of money, she took a reasonably affordable, new car and transformed it into a Gothmobile! See for yourself:

When selecting a Gothic ride, the first and foremost thing to consider is the make and model, as that will dictate the shape of the car. There are some vehicles that you simply aren't going be able to do much with. If you buy a VW Beetle you will probably have to nail a bloody coffin and a dozen skeletons to the roof to make it look like anything less than what it is—a pregnant roller skate.

1) Asia picked the Chrysler PT Cruiser, 2004 Touring Edition as her Goth auto of choice. I will openly admit that originally, I could not look at one of these without imagining the door opening and three midget ZZ Top clowns rolling out of it. Thankfully, though, what she's done with the car has wiped that unappealing vision from my mind forever.

(Oh, yeah—and this photo of Asia helped, too! Wow!)

2) By far, the feature that most loudly and clearly screams "Goth!" is the decal work. Both of the rear passenger windows are accented with white vinyl spider web decals that Asia purchased from *www.neatsigns.com* ($3.25 each!). There are also similar larger designs adorning both of the car's side panels (ordered from *www.awesomedecals.com*; $60.00 for the pair) and twin bats soar opposite one another on the rear windshield (obtained from *www.ultimatedecals.com*; $12.00 each)

Asia applied all of the decals herself with a moderate degree of difficulty. The harder part, she told me, was finding the decals: "I spent many hours hunting them down and emailing several manufacturers to get exactly what I wanted! Still, there are lots of great designs available—bats, skulls, spiders . . . you name it, it can either be found or, if not, you can have it custom made."

She says that people are constantly confusing the decals for something far more complicated; she has heard many shouts of, "Hey, great paintjob!" (perhaps even as many times as the less-appreciated yells of "Nice car, Elvira!").

3) As the appearance of your Gothmobile need not—and should

1

2

not—end with the exterior, Asia decorated the interior of her car to continue the Goth motif within.

3A) She lined the back area of the interior with luxurious red velvet. (I swear it's there . . . somewhere . . . under that, um, nice lady in the photograph). It makes for a very inviting place to . . . "rest."

3B) If you can handle it, the steering wheel is a great spot for some well-placed paraphernalia. Asia covered hers with a spooky black rubber grip with white skulls to keep the Gothic motif right at her fingertips.

3C) Once again Gothic jewelry saves the day! Meant to adorn the body, this necklace of silver bats makes for a fiendishly vampiric ornament around the overhead light. Another necklace featuring a single, large, silver bat hangs in the back window, sending a clear message to all boarding from the rear that they are entering consecrated grounds!

3D) Naturally, dangling from the rear view mirror is a big honkin' skull, just to make sure they see you comin'!

You can just hear the shaken hillbilly's police report: "I swear, officer! I was almost just run down by a skeleton drivin' a creepy, cobweb-covered ZZ Top-lookin' automobile! And then, to add insult to injury, as the car sped off some half-naked, sexy vampire lady in the back gave me the finger!"

4) It takes a lot of thought and effort to transform yourself from a boring Old Navy poster boy/girl to the reigning deity of the underworld. And then there is the issue of names. We Goths often change our names from Jimmy or Susie or Pat to something grimly grandiose, like Dracul or Secretia or Lestat.* Your car deserves nothing less!

*If you still bear a boring, mundane name, see the Gothic Name Generator in *What is Goth?* for some spooky tips.

3a

3b

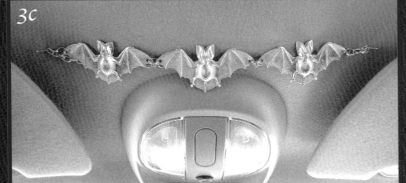

3c

3d

4

*DVINYL

Goth is nothing if not vain—and so, in this spirit, it only makes sense that you spring for a vanity plate. I believe that Asia paid a mere $35 extra for the luxury to sport her name on the license plate of her Gothmobile. Better still, her state even offered a choice of designs that could be added to the plate and in their image bank was a spider! "Thank you Department of Motor Vehicles!!!" The spider goes great with those cobweb decals and is a match made in heaven for the pet name Asia has affection-ately given her car—"Charlotte."

So, there you have it. Start with a nicely shaped, black car, add some dastardly decals and ooky-spooky ornaments and you too can feel like Herman Munster "burnin' though the witches" in your Dragula!

gothic weddings

It's a Nice Day for a . . . Black Wedding!

THE BRIDE IS WEARING WHITE. THE BRIDESMAIDS ARE DECKED OUT IN PASTEL GOWNS. THE GROOM STANDS AT THE ALTAR IN A TUXEDO. OH, LOOK AT THE FLOWER GIRL! SO SWEET IN HER LITTLE, frilly dress, tramping up the aisle. She is scattering delicate flower petals with all of the wonderfully wobbly awkwardness so characteristic of a toddler. After the bride has reached her partner at the pulpit, the pastor begins to speak in solemn tones about love and God and holy matrimony. The parents of the happy couple beam with pride and contentment. They look into the faces of the bride and groom and see there so vividly the true love the two feel for one another. But alas, those expressions have been misread; because in truth, looking into each other's eyes, the communal thought so clearly understood between the partners is, "What the hell are we doing here? This isn't even Goth!"

"I should be wearing a black gown," thinks the bride. "Damn," thinks the groom, "this would have been an excellent occasion for me to pull out my new cape!" The pastor asks, "Do you, Jimmy, take this woman to be your lawfully wedded wife?" The groom cringes. Within the crowd of onlookers, a confused gothic beau turns to his vampiric date, wondering "Did he say, 'Jimmy?' I thought his name was Count Sinestro, Keeper of the Sanguinarians." The pastor continues, "Do you, Tiffany, take this man to be your lawfully wedded husband?" The bride cringes. In the pews there is a faint stir. The surprised vampiric date turns to her gothic beau asking, "Tiffany? I thought her name was Secretia, Defenestrator of the Bats!" Back at the pulpit, some vows are mumbled, rings are exchanged and—in perhaps the most atypical moment of the whole affair—the groom kisses the bride without a single molecule of black lipstick being exchanged between the two.

The couple turns to the congregation of guests and there before them is an aisle leading to the front door of the church. But this aisle seems less like a passageway to their new life together and more like an ominous barrier between two manifestly different groups of people. On the right is a smiling, pastel-wearing horde delighted with the enactment of this wonderfully traditional ceremony. On the left is a fidgety, black mass of gothic guests united in a single thought: "What the *hell* are we doing here? This isn't even Goth!"

A wedding is perhaps the single most important ceremony in the lives of two souls who choose to spend their existences together. Common sense would imply that this ceremony should therefore celebrate the personalities and aesthetics of these two individuals and what they share in common. Sadly and nevertheless, weddings are more often than not planned primarily to satisfy the interests of the couple's parents and their desires to be perceived a certain way by their community. In short, the average parents don't wish to find themselves inviting their family and friends to their daughter's "Dawn of the Dead" theme wedding. Hence, many Goths are coerced into corny, traditional weddings that mean very little to them personally.

These days, more and more intrepid Goths are claiming this most auspicious day for themselves. They are planning Goth weddings that reflect their macabre sensibilities and celebrate their dark aesthetics. They are coming to the unavoidable realization: why have a traditional wedding when you can have funeral for two and invite all of your friends!

WHEN, WHERE, AND MOST IMPORTANTLY, WHO?

Anyone who's ever been married, Goth or not, knows that planning a wedding can be a real pain. Here are some simple tips for taking the sting out of arranging your Goth wedding.

The Gothic Wedding
of
Ian And Shea

Across the board, the most common date for a Gothic wedding is October 31st. Goths love to celebrate their union on their favorite day of the year, Halloween.

Moreover, it's a lot easier to trick your family and friends into attending your Gothic wedding if they think it's a costumed affair. Just picture Grandma, surrounded by a couple hundred Goths, exclaiming, "Isn't this special? Everyone's dressed like a vampire. Oh, the groom is biting the bride's neck instead of kissing her. That's different. Oh look, they're sacrificing a goat! Gosh, that looks so real! Hey . . . wait a minute!"

Where

Ironically, churches make great backdrops for gothic weddings. Really, where better to have a Goth wedding than in a Gothic structure? However, if you're a Protestant Goth you may need to convert to Catholicism fast. Catholics have all of the best churches! And let's face it—chances are, you aren't going to find any gargoyles or statues of tortured saints at the local Protestant house of worship.

Masonic temples and Jewish synagogues also make for great settings. But to secure the former you may need to know a few secret handshakes; and, hell, getting circumcised the day before your honeymoon seems a bit extreme just to gain admittance into the latter.

A castle is a great choice . . . if you can find one. If you ever thought that the United States of America had any sort of ancient history whatsoever, try looking for a castle! It might take some real effort to find an actual palatial structure, unless the idea of getting married next to the fryolator at a White Castle appeals to you (damn, couldn't they at least have called it Black Castle?). You might need to consider going to a country that isn't the equivalent of a cultural toddler, like England, Ireland, Scotland or another place which employs the suffix "land." Still, an intensive enough search might yield a medieval-style reproduction. I officiated the Gothic wedding of my friends Ian and Shea at the Hammond castle in Gloucester, Massachusetts, and I have to say that I was completely bowled over by the sheer beauty of the place—from the Renaissance-styled

Ian Sufa, Voltaire and Guests • Photo: Ryan Speth

dining room to the massive pipe organ. At one point, while standing outside atop the rocky cliffs on which the castle is perched, I had to keep reminding myself that I wasn't at Borgo Pass at Dracula's castle. But hey, I *was* surrounded by a bunch of freaks in capes.

Hardcore Goths might choose to have their wedding in a cemetery, and I've met at least one couple dying to have theirs in a funeral home.

Goth clubs can also be a fun and very economical location for your wedding. For more on that option, read on.

One of the more interesting Goth weddings that I have attended was that of Lord and Lady DJ Wicked Goth in Indianapolis. They held their ceremony outside of their local haunted house (not the kind with real ghosts, mind you; rather, the kind where you pay $10 to go inside and be chased around by teenagers dressed as zombies). Immediately following the "I do's," the couple turned and headed into the haunted house, followed by the entire wedding party, their family, and their friends. It was by far the scariest wedding I have ever attended. But then again, I've never been to a Greek wedding.

Who

If weddings were only attended by the bride, the groom, and an officiator, they'd be easy as pie to plan. But instead, weddings are communal events and are attended (and more often than not paid for) by the bride and groom's family and friends. All of those people may have specific ideas as to what the wedding should be like and even stronger opinions about what it *shouldn't* be like. So, it's no surprise that the single biggest issue in planning a wedding is deciding whom the wedding is *really* for. In other words, how are your parents going to feel about your desire to have a spooky ceremony?

I Love My Parents But They Hate Goth

Most parents are simply not going to go for their son or daughter getting hitched in a funeral home by a guy dressed as Dracula. So, the big question is do your parents respect you and your desires enough to go along with your having a Gothic wedding? If not, then you should ask *yourself,* do you care enough about your parents' desires to concede to a traditional ceremony?

If you do, then the solution is simple. The obvious thing to do is to have two ceremonies: one in black and one in white. One service will be for family and the other for your Goth friends (ironically, the Goth wedding is the one you will view as the "real" one while your parents will see it the other way around).

First let's tackle the "white" wedding. Resign yourself to a traditional ceremony and let your parents make all of the arrangements. White dress? Sure! Demure makeup? Why not? Pink bridesmaid dresses? But of course! You will be astounded at how easy

planning the event becomes when you don't care! Just keep in mind that you are doing this for your parents; this is *their* wedding so let *them* have all of the fun. Also, don't invite the whole damn Goth scene to this one; you'll only feel silly and that will create stress for you. Only invite your closest friends who will understand your altruistic motivations.

Being un-Goth for a day won't kill you and will probably be the biggest gift you'll ever give your parents. So, just sit back, relax, and try to have fun. And if you find yourself beginning to freak out about how tacky, goofy, or terribly un-Goth something is, keep reminding yourself that the "real" wedding is only a few days away and it is going to be the biggest, baddest festival of darkness ever conceived!

THE GOTH CLUB WEDDING

With concerns about the "white" wedding out of the way, it's time to plan your dreadfully dark Gothic wedding!

If your town has a Goth night that you like to frequent, organizing this second wedding will not seem as daunting a task as you may think. Firstly, most Goth promoters—hungry for anything to put on a flyer to promote their night—would be delighted to have you get married at

the club. So right there, the venue is taken care of . . . for *free*!

Secondly, in terms of legal matters, this event is strictly symbolic; therefore, don't worry about finding an actual voodoo priest to do the honors. Have someone in the scene who means a lot to you perform the ceremony. Perhaps a favorite DJ, musician, promoter, or even a particularly spooky friend. And if the cops come, just tell them it's a performance art piece.

As for the guests, invite everyone you know in the scene. Since you are getting married at your local Goth night, most of them will be going there anyway. Moreover, because your dark wedding is part of a pre-existing event, everyone will be expecting to pay the cover and buy themselves drinks at the bar. This eliminates the added expense for you. (Remember, this isn't the ceremony your parents are footing the bill for; the less it costs you, the better.)

If you do happen to have a bunch of disposable income, you can offer to pay the admission price for some or all of the invited guests. Furthermore, while setting up an open bar with the club can be expensive, if it's something you are capable of doing, it's a nice gesture for your friends. But plan it wisely—unless you specifically set the time of the ceremony for very early in the night, chances are you will end up with lots of greedy, pasty-faced strangers drinking your dowry away in an endless stream of Red Devils.

Other details to consider:

Music

You're already at a Goth club, so chances are that the music will be more or less to your taste. Consider giving the DJ a list of requests; but keep in mind that if you are not personally paying him, he is not going to be your private disc-monkey for the night. Also, do not assume that the DJ will have a certain piece of music. If there is a special song you would like to have played during the ceremony or for your first dance with your new spooky spouse, bring a CD with you to give to the DJ. Furthermore, choose something that is soft and instrumental (perhaps something by Dead Can Dance); it will be hard to hear your vows over "This Corrosion" by The Sisters of Mercy.

Band

One thing's for sure—you won't be subjected to a cheesy wedding band. But if there is a specific band that you're especially into, try getting them booked. Mention it to the promoters and see what they think. Offering to cover some of the expenses will improve your chances of having your favorite band play. And try to be realistic. It's highly unlikely that The Cure does weddings. (Then again, there *is* cake!)

Decorations

Here is something on which you should spend a little money. In order to make your Goth club wedding special, the venue (or at least the area where your ceremony will take place) should look different than it usually does. Black streamers or shredded fabric stapled to the ceiling and a couple of dried flower arrangements positioned on waist-high pedestals can help to set the stage.

Cake

Bring a cake to the club. Goths love cake, strangers love cake—hell, everyone loves cake! A fancy Gothic wedding cake decorated in black icing is ideal; or, if you are looking for something less expensive but equally as dramatic, give the Graveyard Cake recipe in this book a try.

Either way, don't get cake on your velvet cape! And stay far away from desserts covered in confectioners' sugar. Then again, it *is* pretty amusing to watch a group of Goths, completely bent over, trying to eat white powdered donuts without getting the pervasive sugary substance on their black velvet finery!

And so, if all goes well, you will have a fabulously spooky wedding surrounded by friends and sympathetic strangers in a place that is familiar and fun and very much to your taste. Moreover, it won't break the bank to pull off. Chances are people will actually buy *you* drinks all night. And that's always a good thing—especially if you've just doomed yourself to being with the same person for the rest of your life.

MY PARENTS ARE UNUSUALLY COOL!

In the unlikely event that your parents love you for who you are and (in the virtually implausible case that they) respect your morbid idiosyncrasies, you may be able to completely forego the dreaded traditional wedding and focus all of your attention (and their cash) on an absolutely fabulous Gothic wedding.

A spooky wedding invitation is a great way to let your guests know what the theme and spirit of the wedding will be. In other words, it should communicate to them what they are getting themselves into! Design a wedding invitation that is dark and elegant and immediately gets the point across: "We are Goths! We love the macabre! And damn it, we're getting married!"

One route to take is to get some black cardstock and handwrite the invitations with a silver marker or calligraphy pen. It's simple, spooky, and can be quite elegant.

Another option is to find yourself a horrific image that can be easily reproduced. For example, I know of one couple who selected a turn-of-the-century horror image from *www.oldfashionhalloween .com* to give their wedding invite that extra-Gothy flair.

Pick a Date

Halloween is a big favorite. If you pick this date, specify on the invitations whether or not you expect your guests to attend in costume. Otherwise, suggest on the invitations that your guests wear something elegant and black. If Aunt Mabel gives you attitude and says something like, "I'm not dressin' like a freakin' vampire! I'm wearing a colorful dress with big, bright flowers on it!" tell her that you are perfectly fine with that; then gently point out that she will be the only person not in black. It's amazing how fast people like that buckle when they believe that they will stand out! After all, it's that very fear that keeps them "normal."

Wedding Dress

When I think "Gothic wedding dress," I picture something classic—in other words, a traditional wedding dress with a veil of flowing lace, but in black. However, there are many other options available to the Gothic bride.

ALLISON • PHOTO FRED BERGER

For the ghoulish gown of your dreams, you can design and sew one yourself or hire a dressmaker to construct it. One lovely Gothic bride, Tina, made her own dress out of vinyl in a style best described as "Victorian meets the 1920s." It was sleek, graceful, and fetishy all at once. Another bride, Allison, took inspiration from a Victorian classic; she had a reproduction of a late-19th Century mourning dress custom made for her. While elegant and dignified, there's no escaping the intrinsic spookiness of a dress designed for anguish!

Some brides choose store-bought dresses or apparel, as there are tons of really cool Goth clothes available out there, if you know where to look. Shea's wedding ensemble (see the photos of her wedding to Ian at the beginning of this chapter) was comprised of a corset and a skirt. The corset was custom-made by Shumit Basu of Underground Aristocracy, with patent leather and matte satin panels and a reflective trim; the skirt, which was vinyl with bustles in the back, was purchased from Lip Service.

At the end of the day, there are many different directions one can take in selecting a Gothic wedding dress. The one thing that will probably be a constant, however, is that it will probably be black. But hey, it's a nice day for a black wedding! Whoo hoo!

Flowers

Bouquets of black roses are the obvious choice. You can sometimes find them in shops that specialize in artificial flowers.

Also, you can use the "Gothic Flower Arranging" section of this book to create some wonderfully wicked arrangements for your gothic wedding. Display them in large black vases adorned with ribbon. A tip: around Halloween time, you can find ribbon that has spooky but tasteful designs (like spider webs); but stay away from Halloween ribbons that have cheesy and gaudy patterns (like bright orange jack-o-lanterns or ghosts yelling, "Boo!").

If you have a flower girl, hand her a basket of dried rose petals to scatter. They are pretty and will make a wonderful crunching sound as you proceed up the aisle. I'm not sure if that's Goth but it sure sounds creepy.

Bridesmaids and Pallbearers

It's important not to overlook the rest of the wedding party in respect to what they will be wearing and how they will appear. They are an extension of you and thus you should make sure that they preserve the theme that you have established for your wedding. If you and your partner are Vampyres, then they should be Vampyres too. If you and your partner are demons, so should it be with them.

Of course, though, a bridesmaid should never overshadow a bride, so try to make the wedding party's outfits "simple but spooky." Perhaps identical, store-bought Gothy dresses for the ladies and tailcoats for the gents.

Also, consider having one person do everyone's makeup. That will give your wedding party a consistent look (especially if they're zombies).

On Compromise

So, we've established that your parents are relatively cool and respect you enough to go along with your Gothic wedding. Nonetheless, you will eventually come to a point at which a compromise will be suggested. The fact is that if there are other people involved, you will probably need to modify your plans slightly so as not to *totally* freak out the "normals." Perhaps your mom isn't crazy about your idea to be in a coffin carried up the aisle by pallbearers (some people are square like that). Or maybe your dad is afraid that his distant relatives from Alabama aren't quite ready for a wedding officiated by three naked witches. Fair enough—he's probably right.

Try to be flexible. So, maybe you leave the wedding in a limousine instead of a hearse. Maybe the three witches could have some clothing on. Give in a little so that Grandma doesn't have a coronary in the middle of the ceremony. Although, you gotta admit that would be awfully memorable . . . not to mention very, very Goth!

Just pick your battles wisely and put your foot down when it comes to the important stuff. You *will* be wearing a black wedding gown, damn it! Anything less would be un-Goth!

MY PARENTS SUCK AND I HATE THEM!

Sing with me: "People . . . people who hate people . . . are the *luckiest* people in the world!!!!"

Ah, love. What a pesky little thing that is. Because when you love people—like, say, your parents—you have to be empathetic and take their wishes and feelings into consideration.

But if they've been right bastards to you your whole life and if you stopped talking to them long ago, then you undoubtedly find yourself with all of the freedom in the world to be as selfish and self-indulgent as you please.

In essence, you want a spooky, Gothic wedding? Go for it, and don't pull any punches! Here's my gothic wedding plan for *you*:

A balmy summer night. (Mostly because I hate the cold and you will too if you're naked!)

An abandoned cathedral somewhere in New Orleans. (Because they sure as hell won't let you pull this off in a functioning church . . . unless they're Unitarians!)

The groom arrives in a horse-drawn carriage. He steps down from it garbed in a top hat and long frock coat, wielding an ornate cane. He is flanked by three vampire concubines whose flowing, transparent gowns of white chiffon flutter in the breeze. The pews are filled with a gothic congregation dressed in their finest Romantigoth attire (no CyberGoths allowed!). The foursome strolls up the candle-lit aisle (in fact, no electricity is allowed either!) to the accompaniment of a gypsy violinist's shrill, stirring refrains. At the altar, a hooded officiator awaits. There is a moment of dramatic silence. Then, another horse-drawn carriage arrives. All look in anticipation. A group of cloaked and masked pallbearers remove a large black coffin from the carriage and proceed up the aisle, moving in step to an ominous dirge played on the enormous pipe organ. All are silent. Once the altar is reached, the coffin is propped upright. The lid is opened to reveal the horrifyingly stunning bride. She is wearing a veil, and little else. Her body is powdered to a pale white. The hooded officiator, adopting a low growl, speaks in a forgotten tongue; his voice conjures up an image of Darth Vader speaking Klingon. He then hands the corpse-bride to the groom and the concubines retreat into the shadowy background. A new, larger coffin is brought to the stage. The groom and his bride step into it. The lid is slammed closed and ferociously nailed shut. The masked pallbearers (who apparently have been working out) lift it onto their shoulders and solemnly carry it to the church door. As soon as they exit, the door is slammed shut, causing a loud, heart-bursting boom, which is intended to represent the termination of the bride and groom's previous lives as individuals . . . but is mostly just to scare the hell out of the wedding guests.

Away from our eyes, the couple (in their coffin) are loaded into a FedEx truck and shipped to Tahiti.

Back inside of the cathedral, a curtain behind the altar opens, revealing a grand orchestra flanking the lone gypsy violinist. They break into *Danse Macabre* by Saint Saens. The pews are pushed to the sides of the room and the dark congregation breaks into a massive communal waltz as wine begins to pour from gargoyle-headed fountains. Someone yells, "release the bats!" A trap door in the floor is opened and up from the catacombs explodes a wave of the flying little monsters. They instantly take to circling the vaulted ceiling. Dark revelry ensues. The night is spent dancing, drinking, sitting, and watching the flying dance of the bats (and trying to not get guano on your tuxedo) and exploring the catacombs by candlelight. Truly a wedding night to remember.

Oh, yeah—and I better be invited!

(My fee for an appearance, you ask? Three vampire concubines and a gallon of blood-wine.)

ALLISON & FRITZ • PHOTO: FRED BERGER

the lair

Pulling It All Together into a Gothic Love Nest

𝕴N THE GOTHIC DECORATING SECTION, WE LEFT YOU WITH A PRIMED CANVAS— MAYBE SOME MAR-VELOUS RED WALLS AND A NICE, SPOOKY BLACK CARPET. AND SINCE THEN, YOU HAVE HAD TIME TO CREATE AND COLLECT MYRIAD GOTHIC ITEMS to help flesh out your abode. Now it's time to put it all together to turn your drab room into a lair of doom. I've chosen a Gothy but classic motif that will scream, "I'm spooky!" while still being charming and subdued enough to not scare off potential dates or give your parents a heart attack when they come to visit.

1) First, hang your curtains—I've chosen a deep purple velvet.

2) Nail some of the flowers you dried earlier directly to the wall for a decorative accent. (I decided to nail them to both sides of the window, thus adding color and interest to what would otherwise be a big, dark, solid space.)

3) String an artificial vine along the curtain rod for further flair and color. (This vine, in autumnal colors, gives the room a sylvan look.)

4) Dress the windowsill with one of your Goth Boxes. Another great aspect to these boxes is that they can hold items inside as well as on top. I chose to have my grimoires framed by the box, and to perch my bottle candelabra on top of it (naturally, this is just for show—you *really* don't want to light candles so close to a big piece of fabric!). Spruce up the remainder of the sill with candles, skulls, Indonesian death boxes, or whatever spooky curios you have lying about.

5) With one windowsill done, move on to the walls. As you've probably noticed by now, I am a big fan of nailing things directly to the wall—whether they are meant to go there or not. Try doing this with a large Indonesian cabinet. Not only will it look great, but it will also offer as a set of drawers right at your fingertips where you can keep your not-so-Gothy items out of sight (paperclips are just so un-Goth!).

6) Here's where the Goth Box really comes in handy: choose a convenient space on the wall and screw the box into place.

7) This box will serve as a great place to display your Gothic dolls; and the top will make a great shelf for candles or other spooky items.

8) Now that you have dispensed with the functional elements, it's time to add some decorative touches. This is your chance to let those spooky picture frames you made fulfill their dark purpose. But what to put in them? Have you ever taken a trip to a graveyard? (What Goth hasn't?) If so, you undoubtedly have wonderful grave rubbings or spooky cemetery shots lying around. Cut some of your grave rubbings to size and put them in your frightening frames. You can also exhibit your phantasmagoric photographing abilities by using enlarged prints (done on your computer or ordered from your local photo lab) of your graveyard photos. If you haven't gotten around to taking uber-Goth shots at a cemetery (what are you waiting for!), pick up some antique, turn-of-the-century photographs at a local thrift store or garage sale. It doesn't matter that they are of strangers as long as they look really really cool!

9) Find a nice empty spot on your wall and fill it with a Gothic cemetery shot or an antique photo in a Gothic picture frame.

10) Finally, nail a cluster of black branches to the wall. You have successfully created a decidedly Gothy section of wall!

11) By this time, your couch should be draped in black fabric and accented with a patterned shawl and cushions. Break up that that big, horizontal, cushiony mass with your Gothic flower arrangement. Place it on an end table behind or beside your couch.

12) Okay, remember that wall that you covered with white curtains? Draw them to the sides and tack them in place on the wall. In the now exposed triangular portion of wall, hang more of your grave rubbings and/or cemetery photos in the remaining Gothic frames. You can also fill in the space with wall-mountable plaster statuary.

13) Now get on the bat phone and call up the hotties, 'cause you have just created a Gothic lair sure to melt the ice off of the reigning prince (or princess) of your local Goth scene.

the last word

A Teary Goodbye
and Some Heartfelt Thanks

ELL, HERE WE ARE AT THE BITTERSWEET END
HOPE YOU HAVE ENJOYED paint it black AND THA
T HAS PROVIDED YOU WITH MANY A HELPFUL TI
N TURNING YOUR MUNDANE SURROUNDING
nto a macabre masterpiece worthy of your Gothic lifestyle. It's
trange world out there, one in which the seemingly unimaginati
nainstream has defined styles of clothing, interior design, musi
nd art that we are all expected to embrace. But we Goths have ou
wn aesthetics, and it seems so terribly unfair that something a
eautiful and as harmless as the styles we love should be so hard t
nd in the stores and malls across America—and furthermore, tha
ur taste in design and fashion should be met with such unreason
ble suspicion and even hatred. I believe that all people should b
ble to pursue their dreams unhampered, so long as they do not hu
nyone. And I sincerely hope that the day will come when Goths an
uppies, Hip-Hoppers and Hippies, Punk-rockers and Preppies (an
es, even Ravers!) can all express themselves creatively and freely, i
ne styles that they respectively love, without having to fear looks c
isdain. It's a big planet and there is plenty of room for everyone t
o their own thing. I don't require that non-Goths like our style;
nly ask that we be given room to be ourselves (and maybe in retur
'e can promise to not make fun of them for being boring!).

In the process of making this book, I have found myself repeatedl
xplaining to people my objective. "It's a Gothic homemakin
ook," I would tell them. More often than not, I would get th
esponse, "Oh! So, you're like the Gothic Martha Stewart?" An
hile I have found that notion amusing, I have been quick to inforn
nem that that title is already taken. There has been a "Gothi
Iartha Stewart" site on the Internet for years that I have heal

people mention from time to time. I therefore feel I should tip my top hat to those intrepid folks for providing the spooky denizens of the Goth scene with devious decorating tips long before I thought to put out a Gothic homemaking book. To them, I raise my Red Devil and say, "Salut!" For those of you interested in checking out their site, simply type "Gothic Martha Stewart" into any web search engine and you will be directed to their virtual doorstep.

I would also like to take a moment to tip my hat to Hot Topic. If you live in Manhattan or Los Angeles or London, etc., chances are that you have an area of town (like New York City's St. Mark's Place) where you can go to stock up on Punk apparel, Gothic accessories, Raver gear, etc. But if you live anywhere in between, it is damned near impossible to find anything whatsoever with a counterculture aesthetic! Popping up in malls across America, Hot Topic has filled that void; it has provided kids in the creative wastelands of suburbia with access to clothes or toys or accessories that are within the genre. If you are someone who hops into a car and drives twelve hours to the nearest major city to find counterculture items that are somewhat more obscure, then I suppose that you perhaps deserve some sort of praise. But please, lay off of the less fortunate souls who don't drive and are stuck in the suburbs. As a final note on this topic, I relate this: I grew up in the suburbs, where my family still lives, and to this day it has been impossible for them to buy me *any* gift that doesn't get directly donated to the Salvation Army the second I return to Manhattan. But now that there's a Hot Topic at their local mall, I can tell them, "Just get me something from there." At least I know it will be spooky.

If there were a Hot Topic at the mall when I was growing up, I can confidently say that my life would have been measurably less miserable.

Lastly, I would like to say that this book was done with the help of certain people who generously gave of themselves to make it possible. The folks at Weiser Books deserve great thanks for their support, for their patience, and for making this book a reality. Thanks also go to my friend Dave Fooden (or Darkwave Dave, as we like to call him) for helping tremendously with the layout. A big hug to my pal Nicholai for being there, camera in hand, whenever necessary.

And eternal thanks to my partner and best friend Oddree for being the best damned editor I've ever met. Every word I wrote in this book was edited by her before being sent the publisher; and let me tell you that without her, I would not sound anywhere near as eloquent as I appear. To prove it, I will insist that she not edit this next sentence (okay Oddree?). "Making like Goffic stuf is totaly like kewl!!. Thanks you four meeking me sound lik I tok so purty!" (Okay, you can edit now). My abecedarian endeavors in the realm of literary pursuits have been greatly augmented to Brobdingnagian proportions due to your divine interventions! And for that, I thank thee!

Thanks to all of my friends online who so readily came to my aid when I had questions or was in need of a photo. I truly appreciate your unending enthusiasm and willingness to lend a hand and I deeply apologize if your contributions did not make it into the book. Your gestures of kindness will not be forgotten!

Lastly, thank *you*, the reader, for spending some time with me and for allowing me into your home to share my kooky insights on spooky decorating. I hope you have enjoyed our little sojourn and I look forward to sharing time with you again in the future!

Feel free to contact me at Voltaire@voltaire.net.
I look forward to hearing your thoughts!

Stay Spooky!

Voltaire
www.voltaire.net